THE LONG ROAD HOME

Recent Doonesbury Books by G. B. Trudeau

Virtual Doonesbury
Planet Doonesbury
Buck Wild Doonesbury
Duke 2000: Whatever It Takes
The Revolt of the English Majors
Peace Out, Dawg!
Got War?
Talk to the Hand

Anthologies

The Doonesbury Chronicles
Doonesbury's Greatest Hits
The People's Doonesbury
Doonesbury Dossier: The Reagan Years
Doonesbury Deluxe: Selected Glances Askance
Recycled Doonesbury: Second Thoughts on a Gilded Age
The Portable Doonesbury
The Bundled Doonesbury

Special Collections

Flashbacks: Twenty-Five Years of Doonesbury
Action Figure!: The Life and Times of Doonesbury's Uncle Duke

THE LONG ROAD HOME

One Step at a Time

A Doonesbury Book
by G. B. TRUDEAU

**Andrews McMeel
Publishing, LLC**
Kansas City • Sydney • London

DOONESBURY is distributed internationally by Universal Press Syndicate.

Andrews McMeel Publishing, LLC
an Andrews McMeel Universal company
1130 Walnut Street, Kansas City, Missouri 64106

13 14 15 16 17 BBG 10 9 8 7 6

ISBN: 978-0-7407-5385-5

Library of Congress Control Number: 2004116364

DOONESBURY may be viewed on the Internet at
www.doonesbury.com and www.ucomics.com.

The author extends his thanks to Jann Wenner for his kind permission to reprint the front and back cover art, which orginally appeared in *Rolling Stone*.

You can't say civilization don't advance, for in
every war they kill you in a new way.
—Will Rogers

Foreword
by Senator John McCain

It has become a cliché to say that American soldiers take the greatest risks in our name and make the ultimate sacrifices for our country. But take a minute and think about it. When most of us go to work, a tough day on the job means a missed meeting or too many calls, maybe a difficult colleague or a terrible commute. When our men and women in uniform have a rough day, it can mean an exploded Humvee, the death of a dear friend, the loss of a limb, or another grievous wound.

And yet in the many years I have spent among wounded soldiers, I know that their experiences are not merely heartrending—each one is also an inspiration. Injuries deprive a solider of more than health alone, and though his life may change in an instant, the rebuilding process can take years. His wounds may render him dependent on doctors and family; they may strip him of all familiarity and leave him with a radically new way to live. But every time I speak with a wounded soldier, I am struck most by what wounds do not harm. The spirit and drive that urged our soldiers into uniform and into the fight never seem to wane. As these brave men and women struggle to heal, often in pain and depression, they nearly always express an undiminished desire to return to their comrades-in-arms and serve their country.

This is the story of thousands of American soldiers, and it is also the tale of B.D., the *Doonesbury* character who loses his leg in an explosion near Fallujah. As B.D. leaves Iraq and begins the long road of recovery at Walter Reed Medical Center, his wife, daughter, and friend go to Fisher House—the facility that has served as a "home away from home" for more than 65,000 military families across the country. Fisher Houses, located on the grounds of every major military medical center, enable family members to be close to the wounded during their hospitalization. As war veterans rebuild their bodies and their lives, the presence of their loved ones is absolutely invaluable.

In this book, Garry Trudeau tells the story of B.D.—and of Fisher House—and he does it very, very well. Biting but never cynical, and often wickedly funny, these comic strips will make you laugh, reflect, and—in the end—understand. Like B.D., the thousands of soldiers who have left their health or their limbs on the battlefield have done so in the service of all of us. These brave men and women astonish us all with their spirit. In sacrificing themselves, they sacrifice for us.

THE LONG ROAD HOME

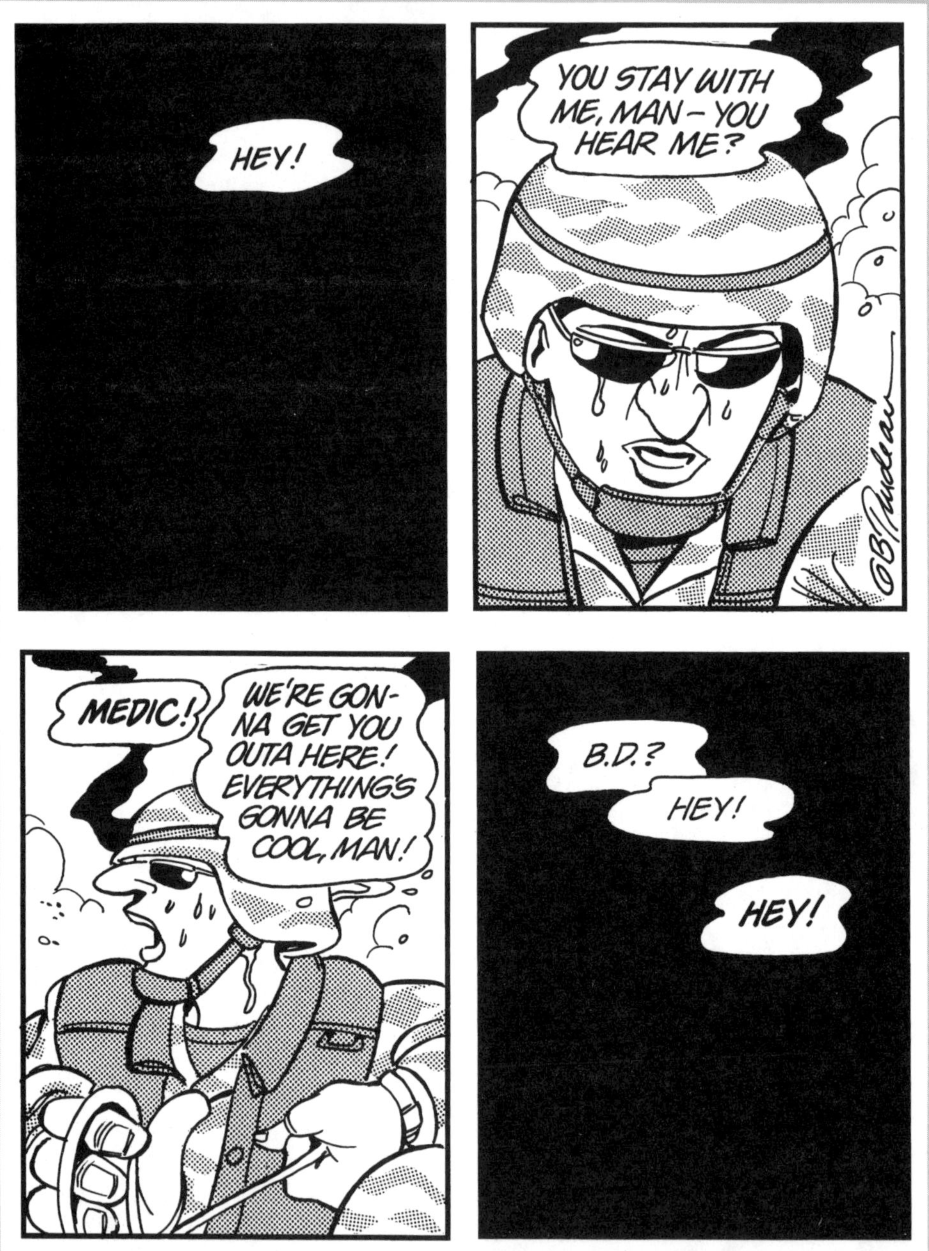
HEY!
YOU STAY WITH ME, MAN – YOU HEAR ME?
MEDIC!
WE'RE GONNA GET YOU OUTA HERE! EVERYTHING'S GONNA BE COOL, MAN!
B.D.?
HEY!
HEY!

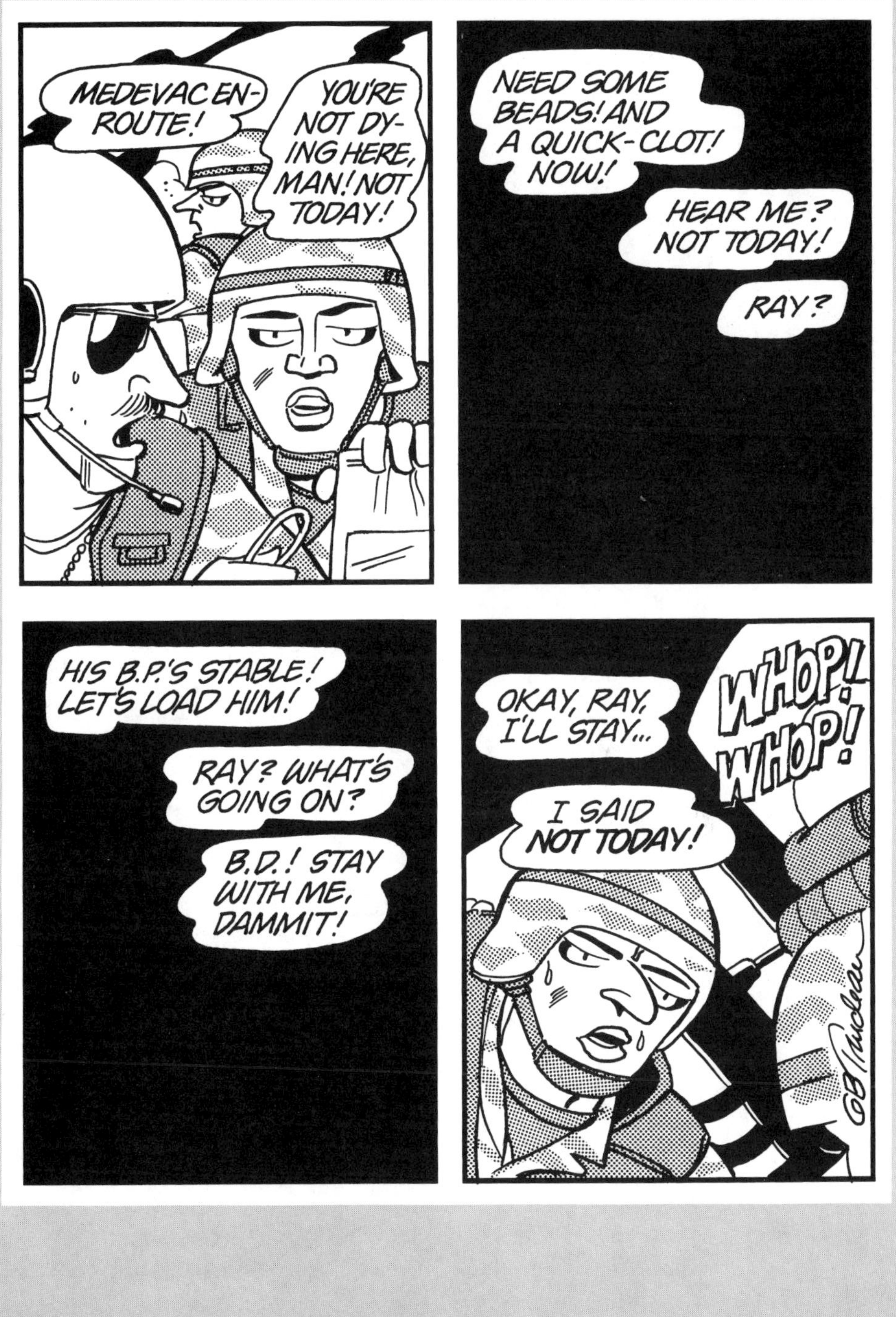
MEDEVAC EN-ROUTE!
YOU'RE NOT DY-ING HERE, MAN! NOT TODAY!
NEED SOME BEADS! AND A QUICK-CLOT! NOW!
HEAR ME? NOT TODAY!
RAY?
HIS B.P.'S STABLE! LET'S LOAD HIM!
RAY? WHAT'S GOING ON?
B.D.! STAY WITH ME, DAMMIT!
OKAY, RAY, I'LL STAY...
WHOP! WHOP!
I SAID NOT TODAY!

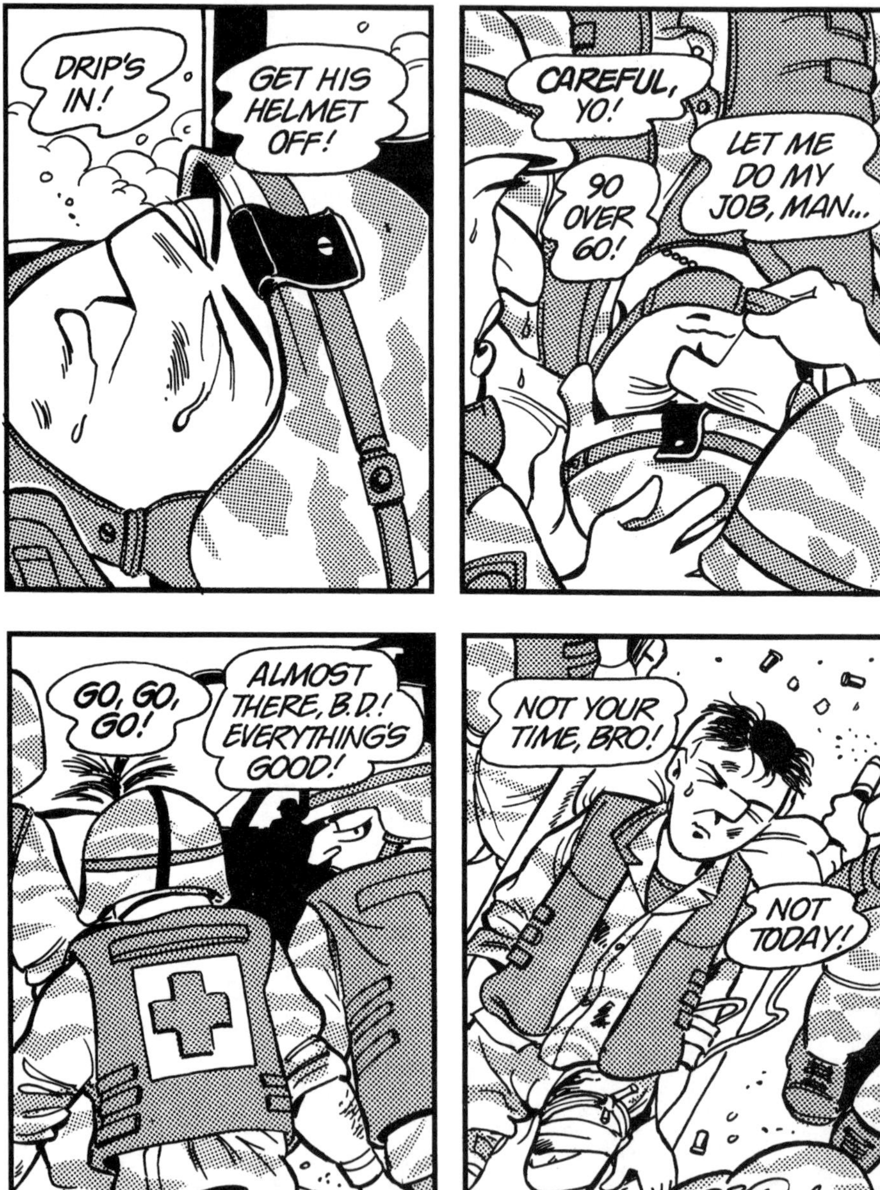
DRIP'S IN!
GET HIS HELMET OFF!
CAREFUL, YO!
90 OVER 60!
LET ME DO MY JOB, MAN...
GO, GO, GO!
ALMOST THERE, B.D.! EVERYTHING'S GOOD!
NOT YOUR TIME, BRO!
NOT TODAY!
©B Trudeau

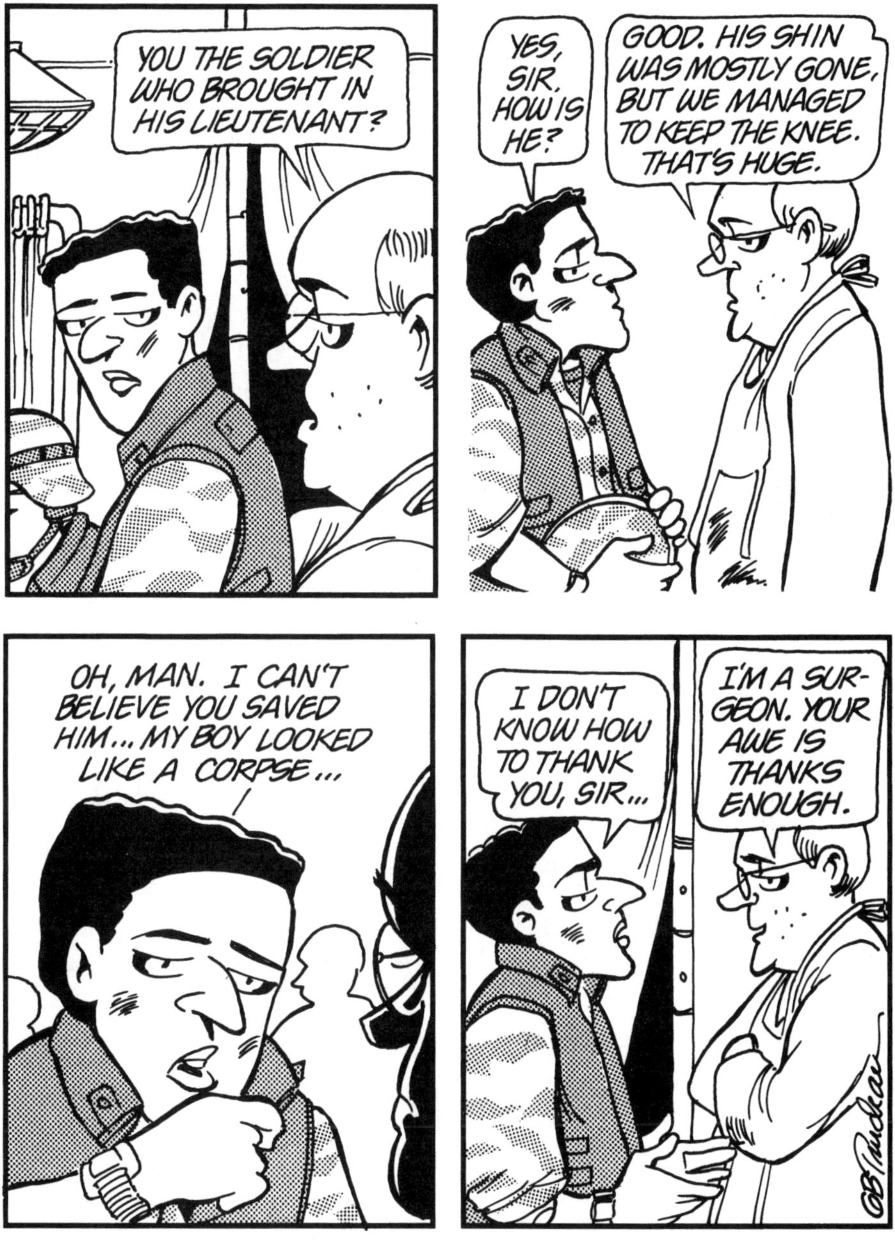
YOU THE SOLDIER WHO BROUGHT IN HIS LIEUTENANT?
YES, SIR. HOW IS HE?
GOOD. HIS SHIN WAS MOSTLY GONE, BUT WE MANAGED TO KEEP THE KNEE. THAT'S HUGE.
OH, MAN. I CAN'T BELIEVE YOU SAVED HIM... MY BOY LOOKED LIKE A CORPSE...
I DON'T KNOW HOW TO THANK YOU, SIR...
I'M A SURGEON. YOUR AWE IS THANKS ENOUGH.
GBTrudeau

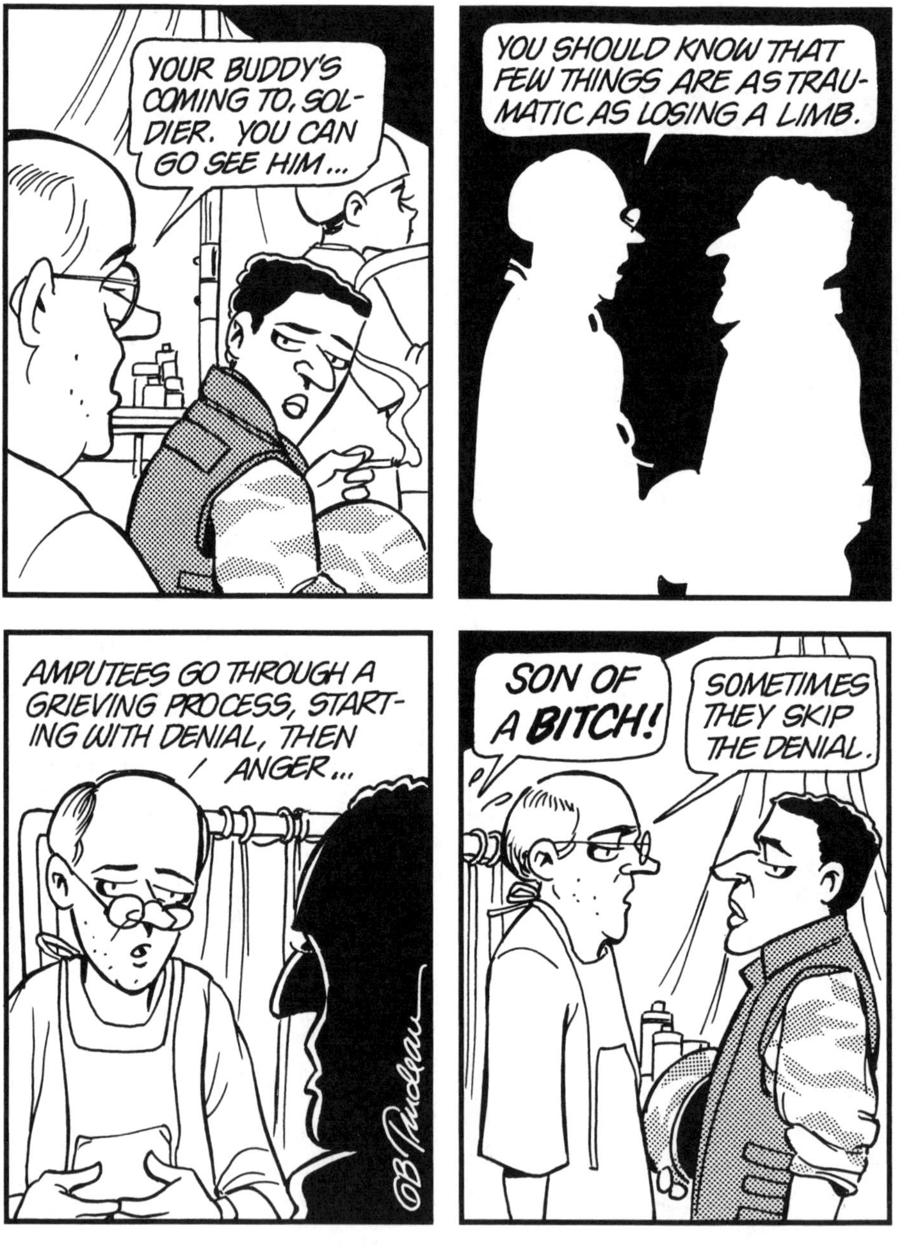
YOUR BUDDY'S COMING TO, SOL- DIER. YOU CAN GO SEE HIM...
YOU SHOULD KNOW THAT FEW THINGS ARE AS TRAU- MATIC AS LOSING A LIMB.
AMPUTEES GO THROUGH A GRIEVING PROCESS, START- ING WITH DENIAL, THEN ANGER...
©B Trudeau
SON OF A BITCH!
SOMETIMES THEY SKIP THE DENIAL.

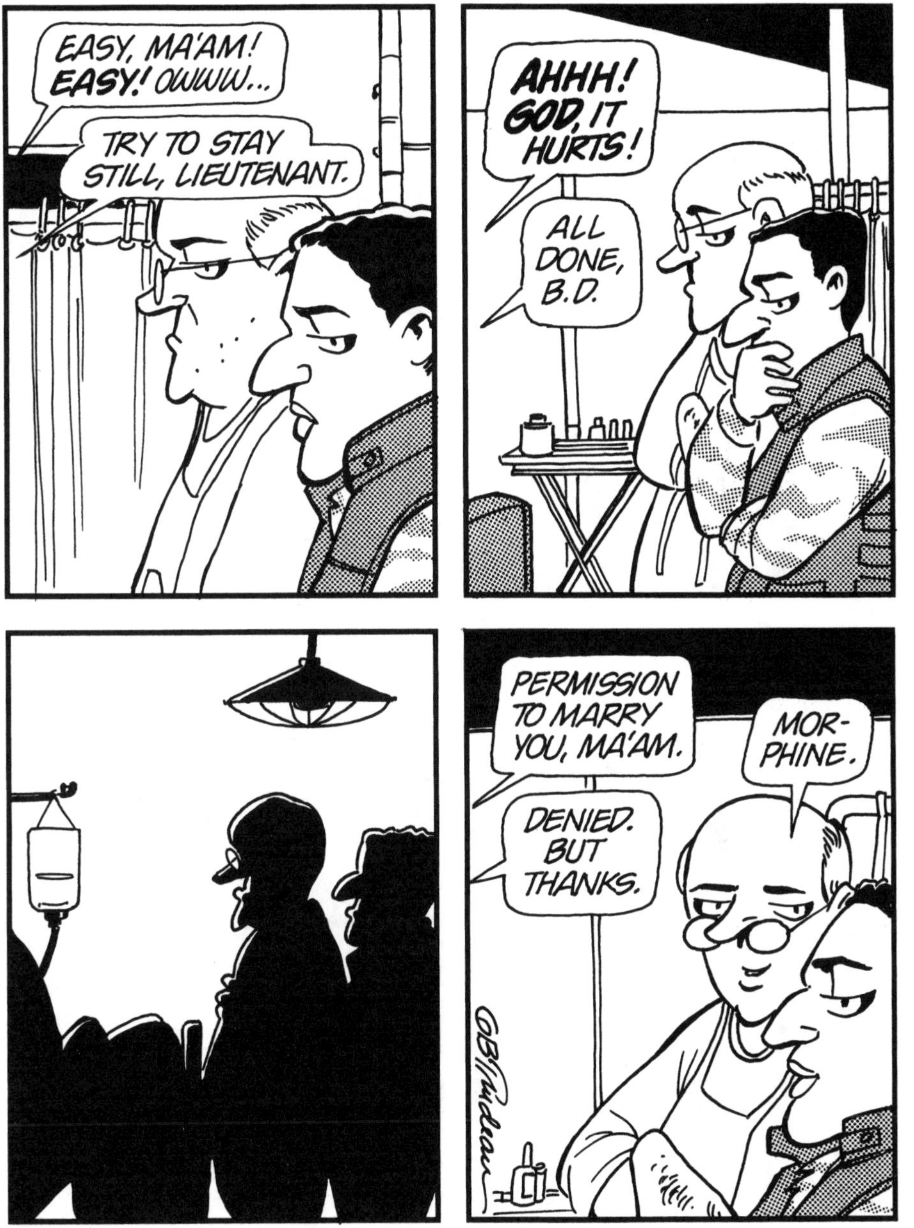
EASY, MA'AM! EASY! OWWW...
TRY TO STAY STILL, LIEUTENANT.
AHHH! GOD, IT HURTS!
ALL DONE, B.D.
PERMISSION TO MARRY YOU, MA'AM.
MOR-PHINE.
DENIED. BUT THANKS.
GBTrudeau

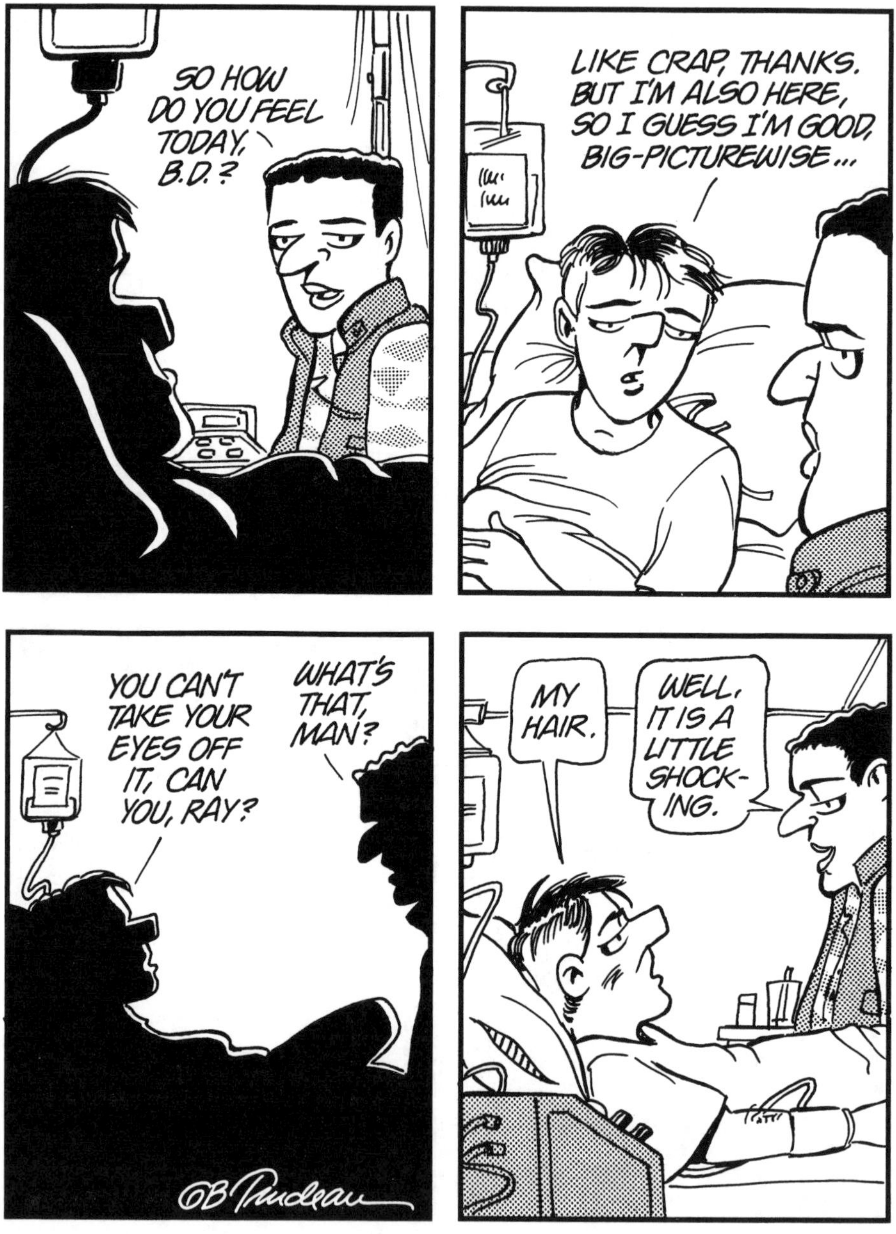
SO HOW DO YOU FEEL TODAY, B.D.?
LIKE CRAP, THANKS. BUT I'M ALSO HERE, SO I GUESS I'M GOOD, BIG-PICTUREWISE...
YOU CAN'T TAKE YOUR EYES OFF IT, CAN YOU, RAY?
WHAT'S THAT, MAN?
MY HAIR.
WELL, IT IS A LITTLE SHOCKING.
©B Trudeau

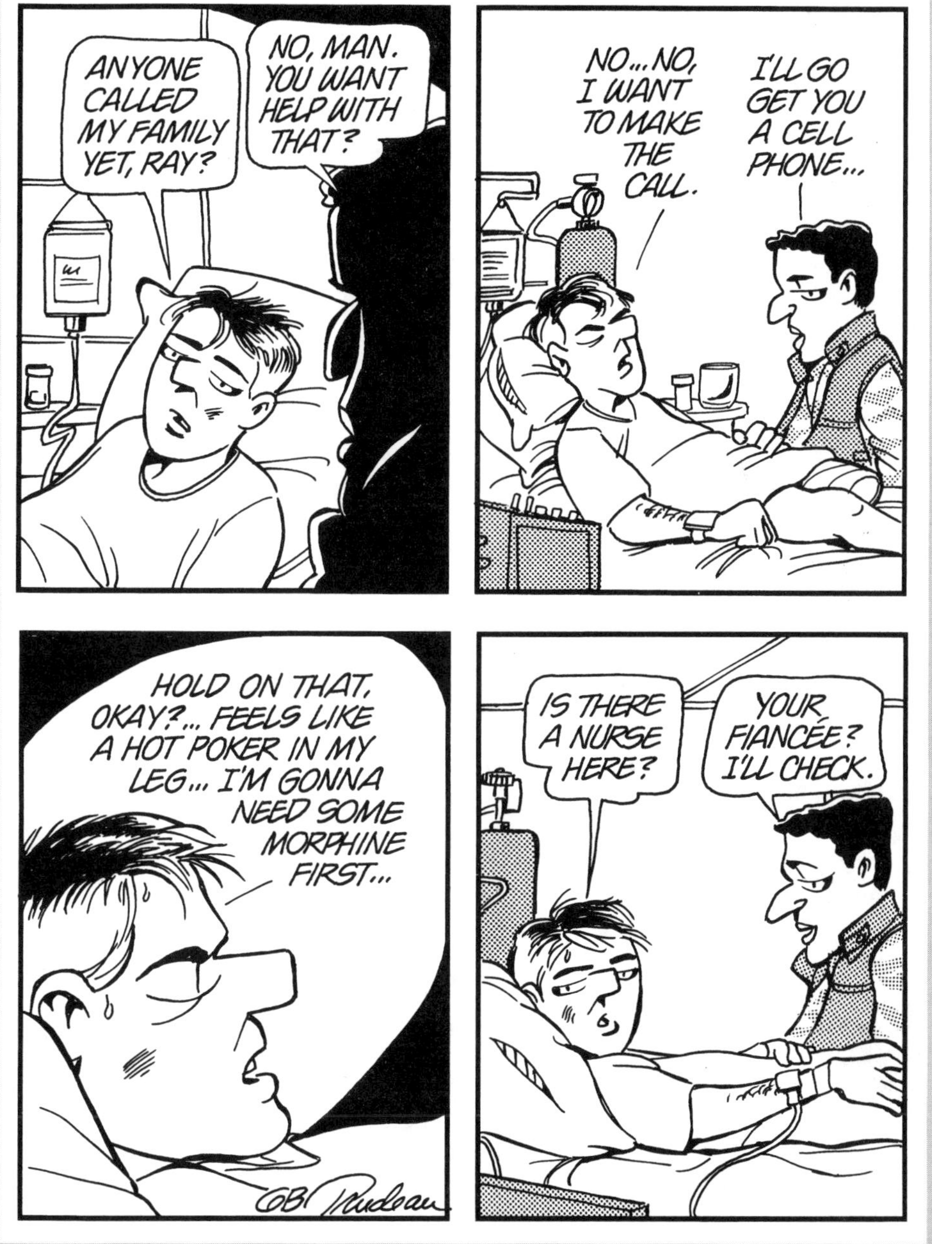

ANYONE CALLED MY FAMILY YET, RAY?
NO, MAN. YOU WANT HELP WITH THAT?
NO... NO, I WANT TO MAKE THE CALL.
I'LL GO GET YOU A CELL PHONE...
HOLD ON THAT, OKAY?... FEELS LIKE A HOT POKER IN MY LEG... I'M GONNA NEED SOME MORPHINE FIRST...
IS THERE A NURSE HERE?
YOUR FIANCÉE? I'LL CHECK.

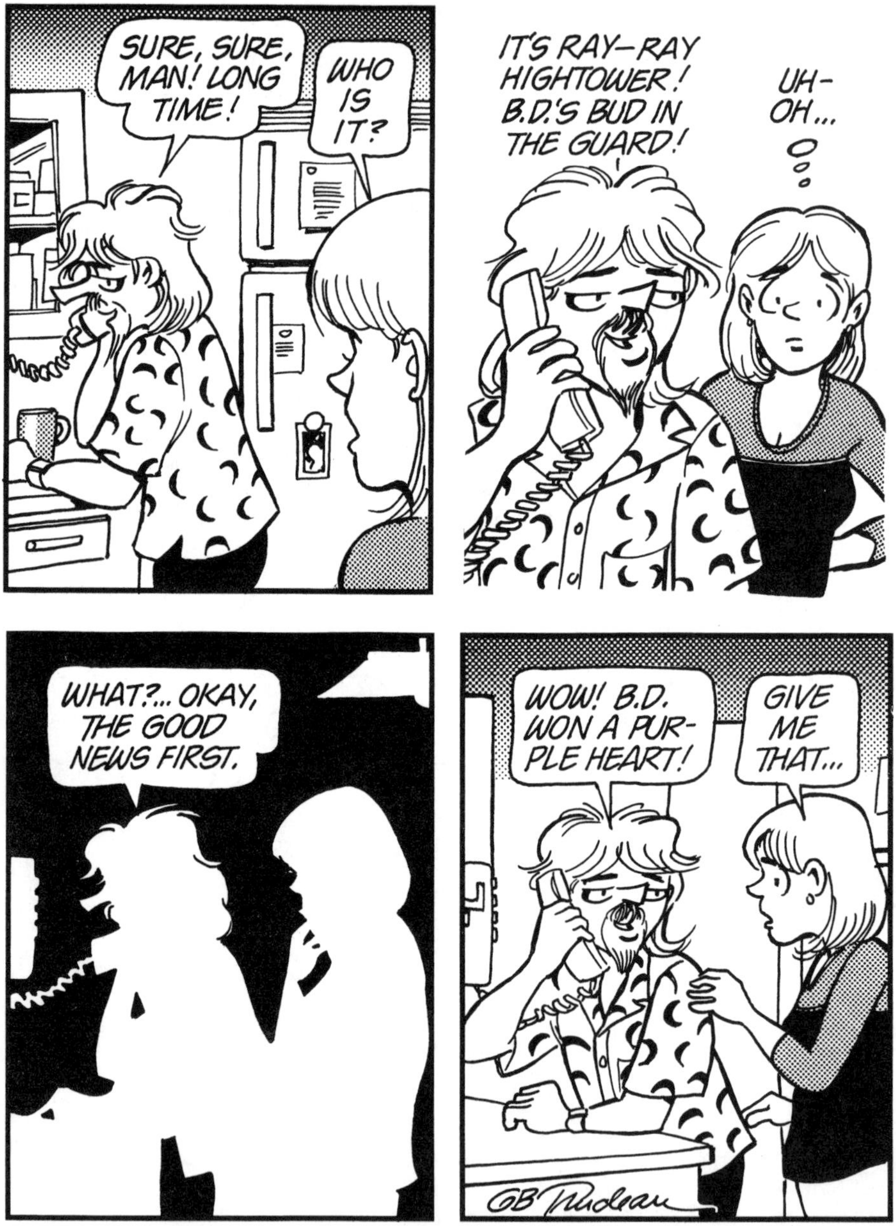
SURE, SURE, MAN! LONG TIME!
WHO IS IT?
IT'S RAY-RAY HIGHTOWER! B.D.'S BUD IN THE GUARD!
UH-OH...
WHAT?... OKAY, THE GOOD NEWS FIRST.
WOW! B.D. WON A PURPLE HEART!
GIVE ME THAT...

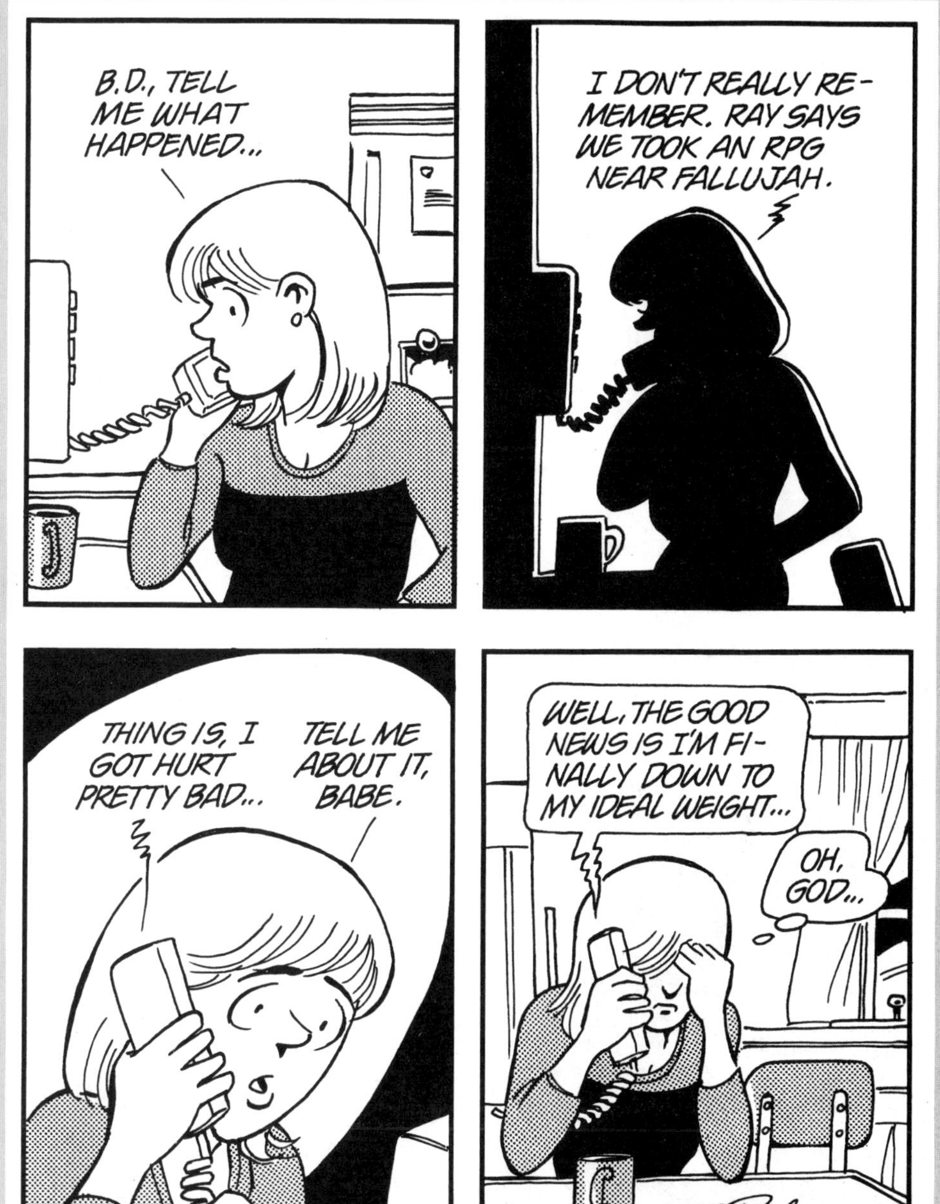
B.D., TELL ME WHAT HAPPENED...
I DON'T REALLY REMEMBER. RAY SAYS WE TOOK AN RPG NEAR FALLUJAH.
THING IS, I GOT HURT PRETTY BAD...
TELL ME ABOUT IT, BABE.
WELL, THE GOOD NEWS IS I'M FINALLY DOWN TO MY IDEAL WEIGHT...
OH, GOD...
©B Trudeau

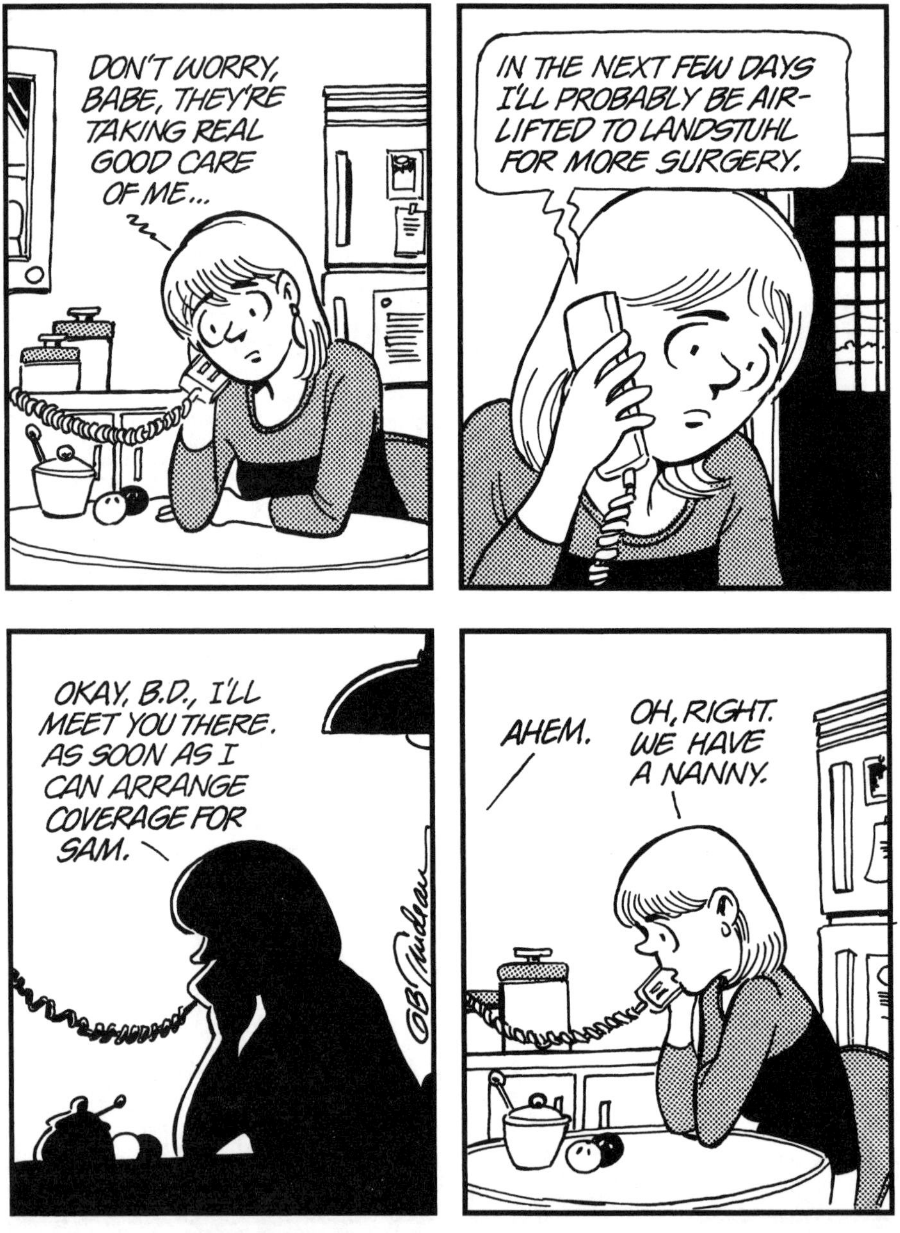
DON'T WORRY, BABE, THEY'RE TAKING REAL GOOD CARE OF ME...
IN THE NEXT FEW DAYS I'LL PROBABLY BE AIR-LIFTED TO LANDSTUHL FOR MORE SURGERY.
OKAY, B.D., I'LL MEET YOU THERE. AS SOON AS I CAN ARRANGE COVERAGE FOR SAM.
AHEM.
OH, RIGHT. WE HAVE A NANNY.

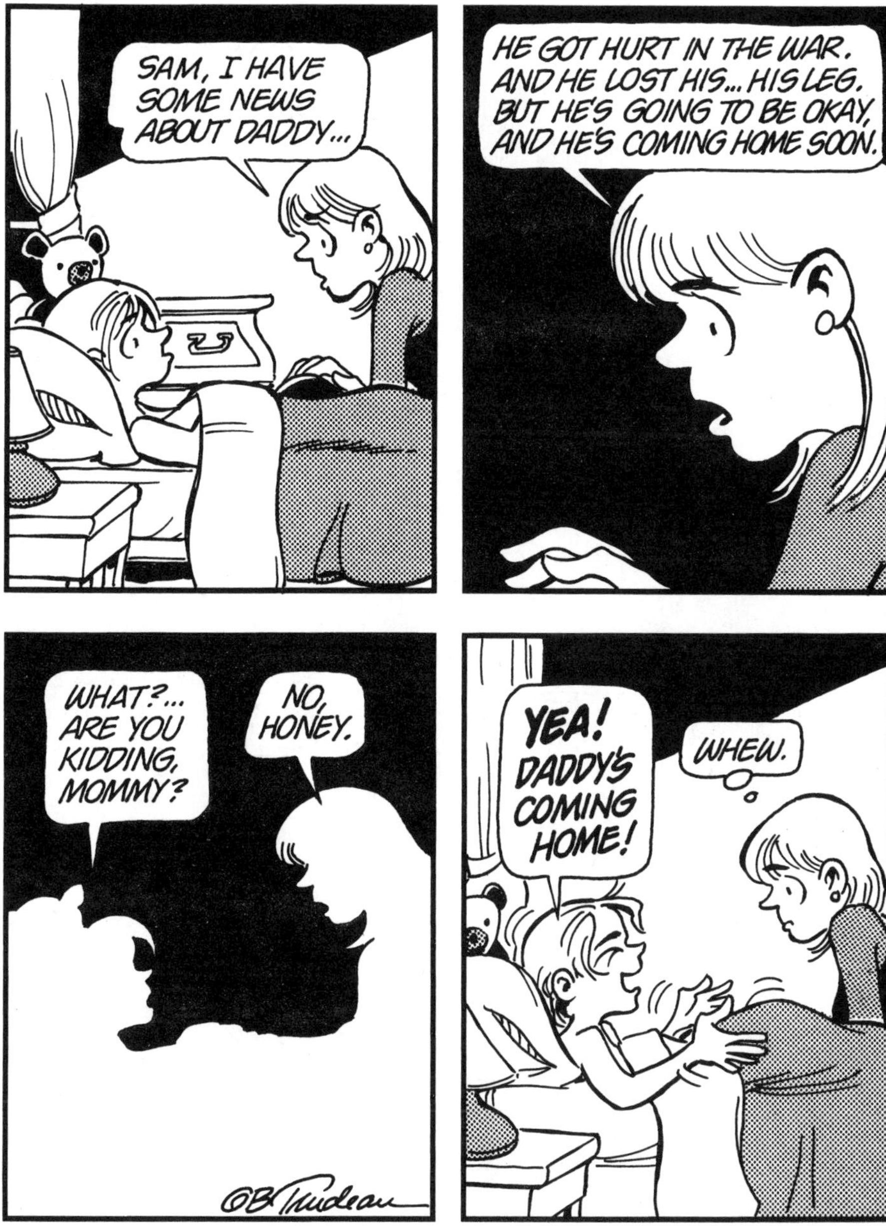
SAM, I HAVE SOME NEWS ABOUT DADDY...
HE GOT HURT IN THE WAR. AND HE LOST HIS... HIS LEG. BUT HE'S GOING TO BE OKAY, AND HE'S COMING HOME SOON.
WHAT?... ARE YOU KIDDING, MOMMY?
NO, HONEY.
©B. Trudeau
YEA! DADDY'S COMING HOME!
WHEW.

GOOD MORNING, LIEUTENANT. WELCOME TO LANDSTUHL!
I'M DR. SPRATT. I'LL BE OVERSEEING YOUR TREAT-MENT HERE AT THE WAR-RIOR CARE CENTER.
GOOD TO MEET YOU, DOCTOR. SAY HELLO TO MY RAGGEDY LEFT LEG...
UH... HELLO.
AND MY BEAU-TIFUL RIGHT HAND.
HI!
©B Trudeau

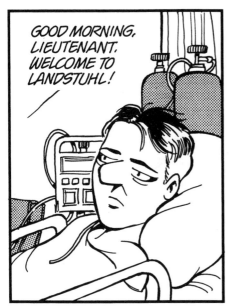

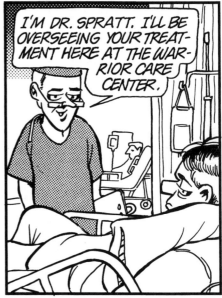

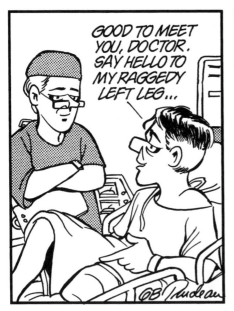

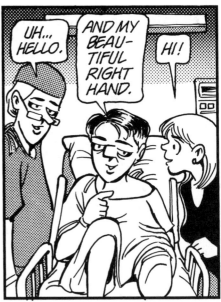

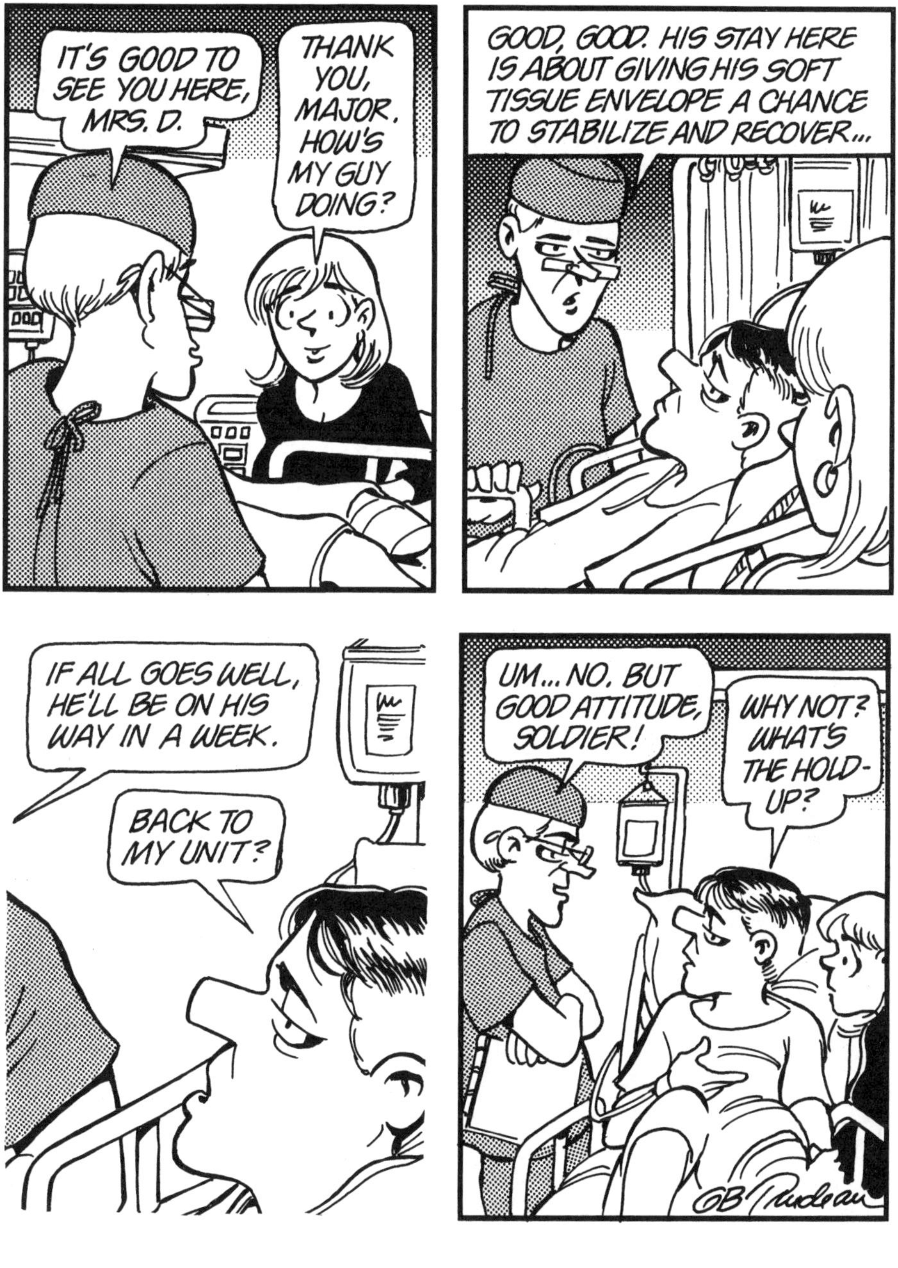
IT'S GOOD TO SEE YOU HERE, MRS. D.
THANK YOU, MAJOR. HOW'S MY GUY DOING?
GOOD, GOOD. HIS STAY HERE IS ABOUT GIVING HIS SOFT TISSUE ENVELOPE A CHANCE TO STABILIZE AND RECOVER...
IF ALL GOES WELL, HE'LL BE ON HIS WAY IN A WEEK.
BACK TO MY UNIT?
UM... NO. BUT GOOD ATTITUDE, SOLDIER!
WHY NOT? WHAT'S THE HOLD-UP?
GB Trudeau

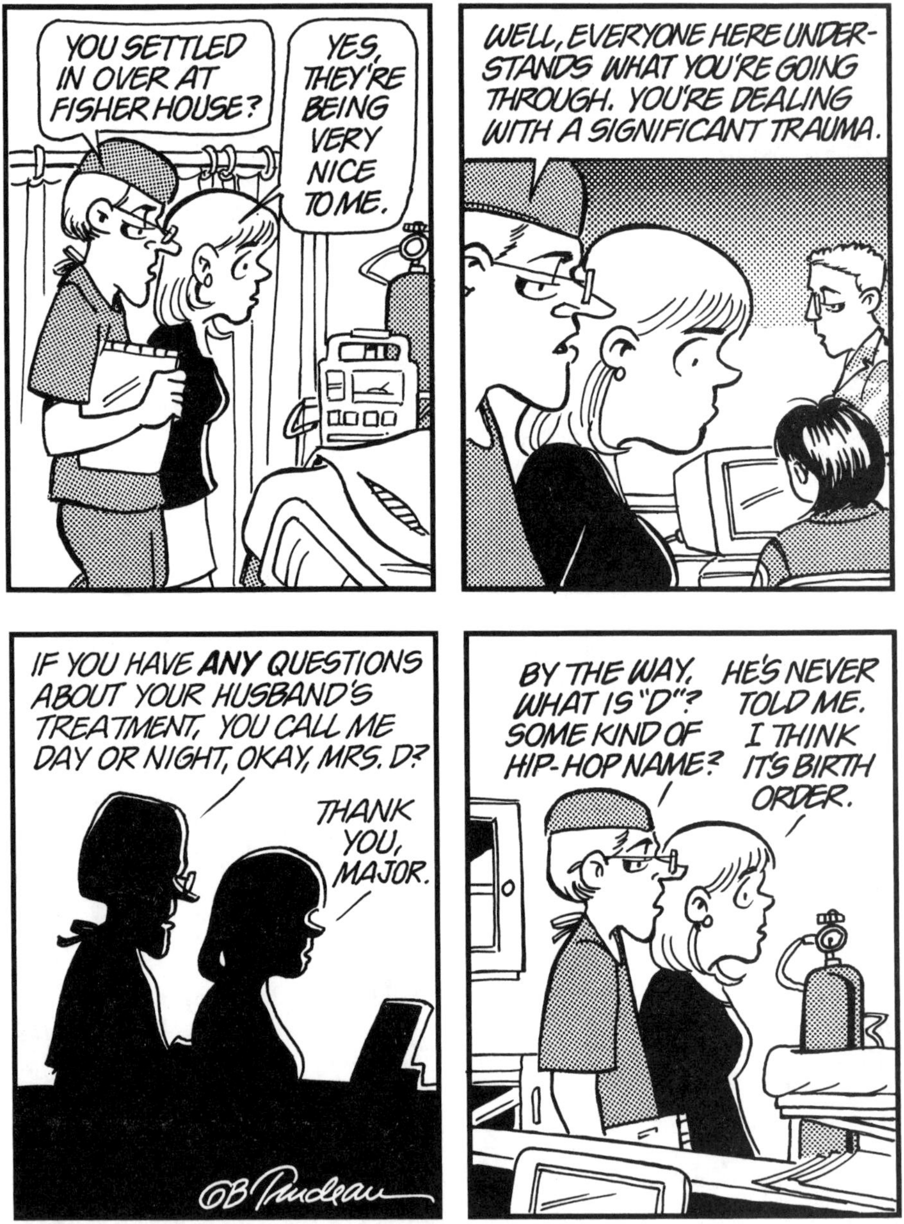
YOU SETTLED IN OVER AT FISHER HOUSE?
YES, THEY'RE BEING VERY NICE TO ME.
WELL, EVERYONE HERE UNDER-STANDS WHAT YOU'RE GOING THROUGH. YOU'RE DEALING WITH A SIGNIFICANT TRAUMA.
IF YOU HAVE **ANY** QUESTIONS ABOUT YOUR HUSBAND'S TREATMENT, YOU CALL ME DAY OR NIGHT, OKAY, MRS. D?
THANK YOU, MAJOR.
BY THE WAY, WHAT IS "D"? SOME KIND OF HIP-HOP NAME?
HE'S NEVER TOLD ME. I THINK IT'S BIRTH ORDER.
©B Trudeau

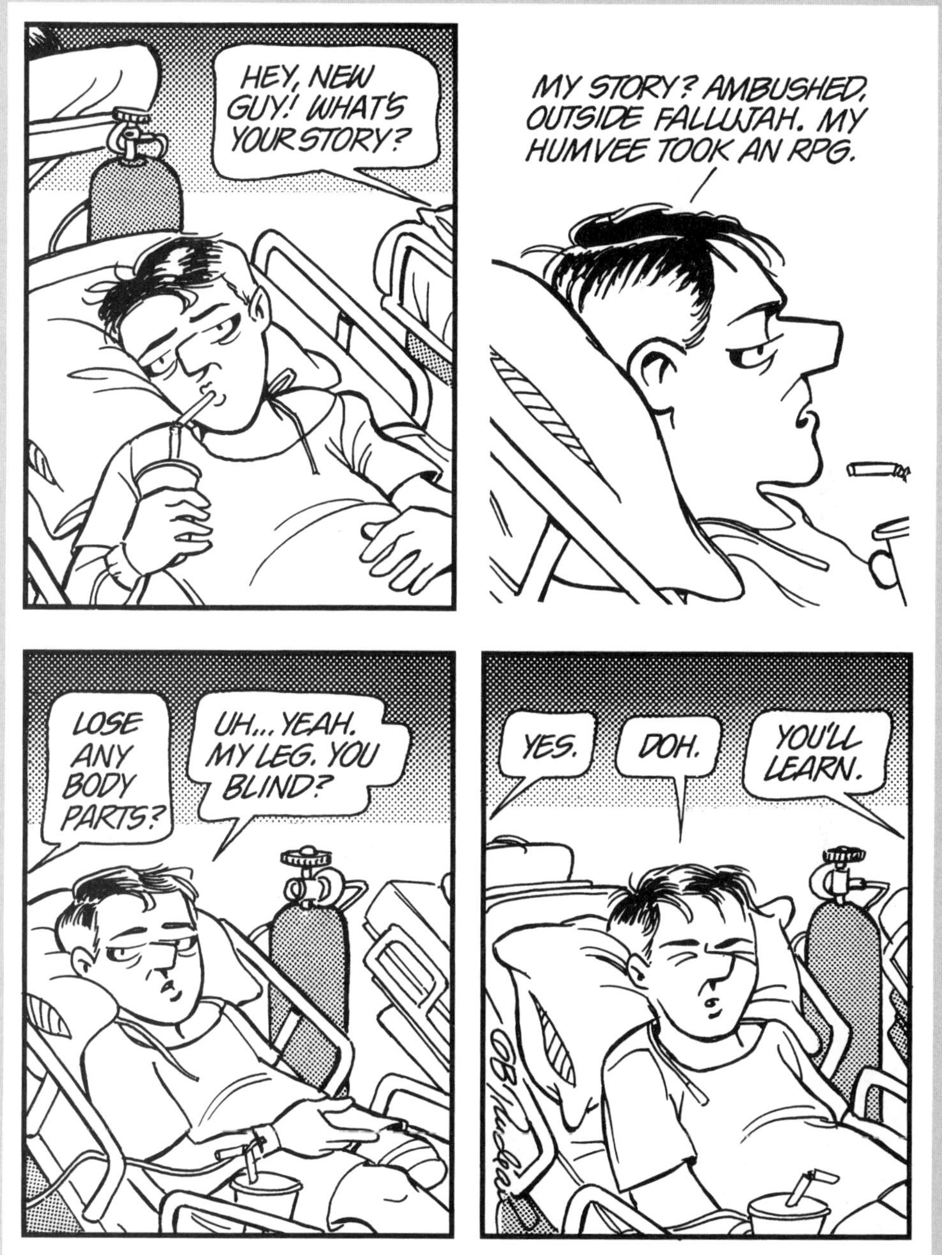
HEY, NEW GUY! WHAT'S YOUR STORY?
MY STORY? AMBUSHED, OUTSIDE FALLUJAH. MY HUMVEE TOOK AN RPG.
LOSE ANY BODY PARTS?
UH... YEAH. MY LEG. YOU BLIND?
YES.
DOH.
YOU'LL LEARN.

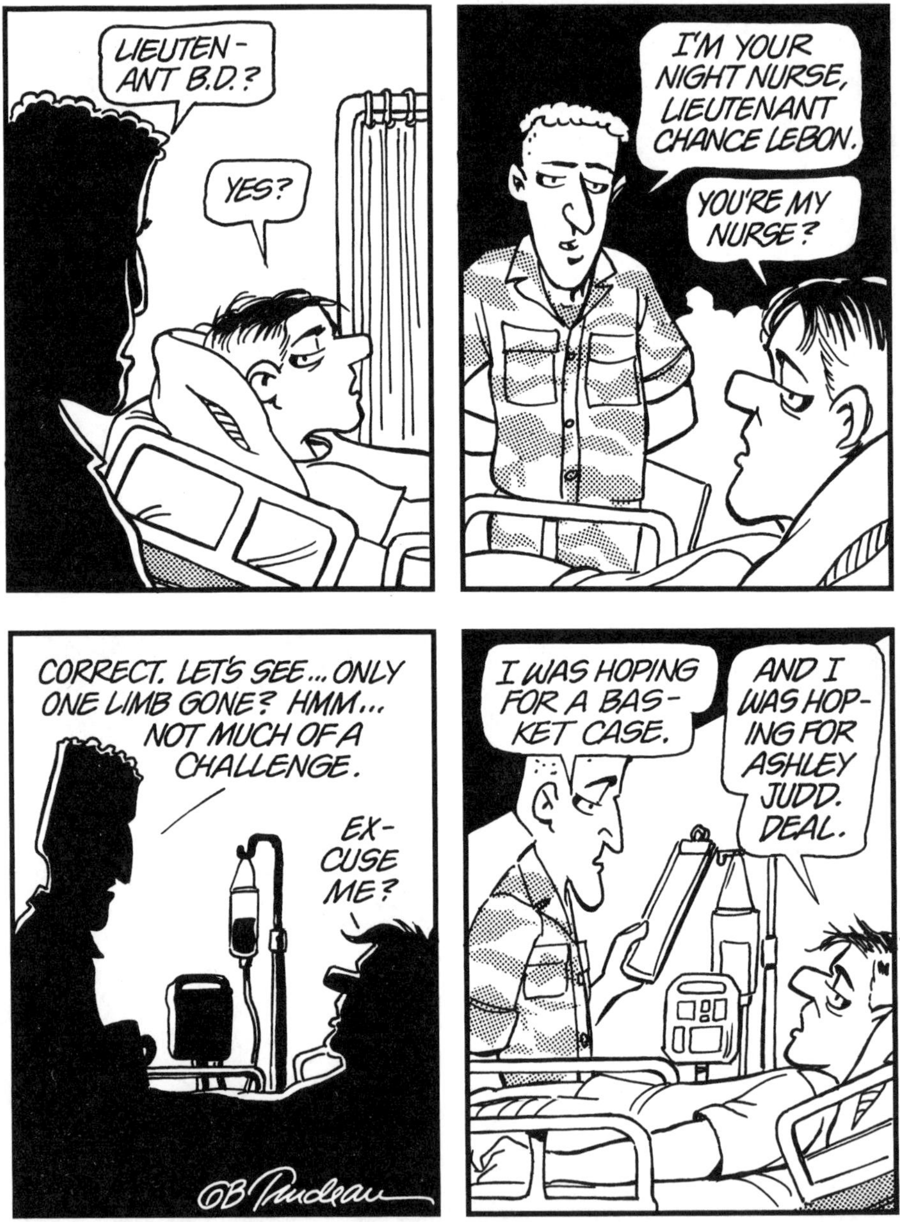
LIEUTEN-ANT B.D.?
YES?
I'M YOUR NIGHT NURSE, LIEUTENANT CHANCE LEBON.
YOU'RE MY NURSE?
CORRECT. LET'S SEE... ONLY ONE LIMB GONE? HMM... NOT MUCH OF A CHALLENGE.
EX-CUSE ME?
I WAS HOPING FOR A BAS-KET CASE.
AND I WAS HOP-ING FOR ASHLEY JUDD. DEAL.
©B Trudeau

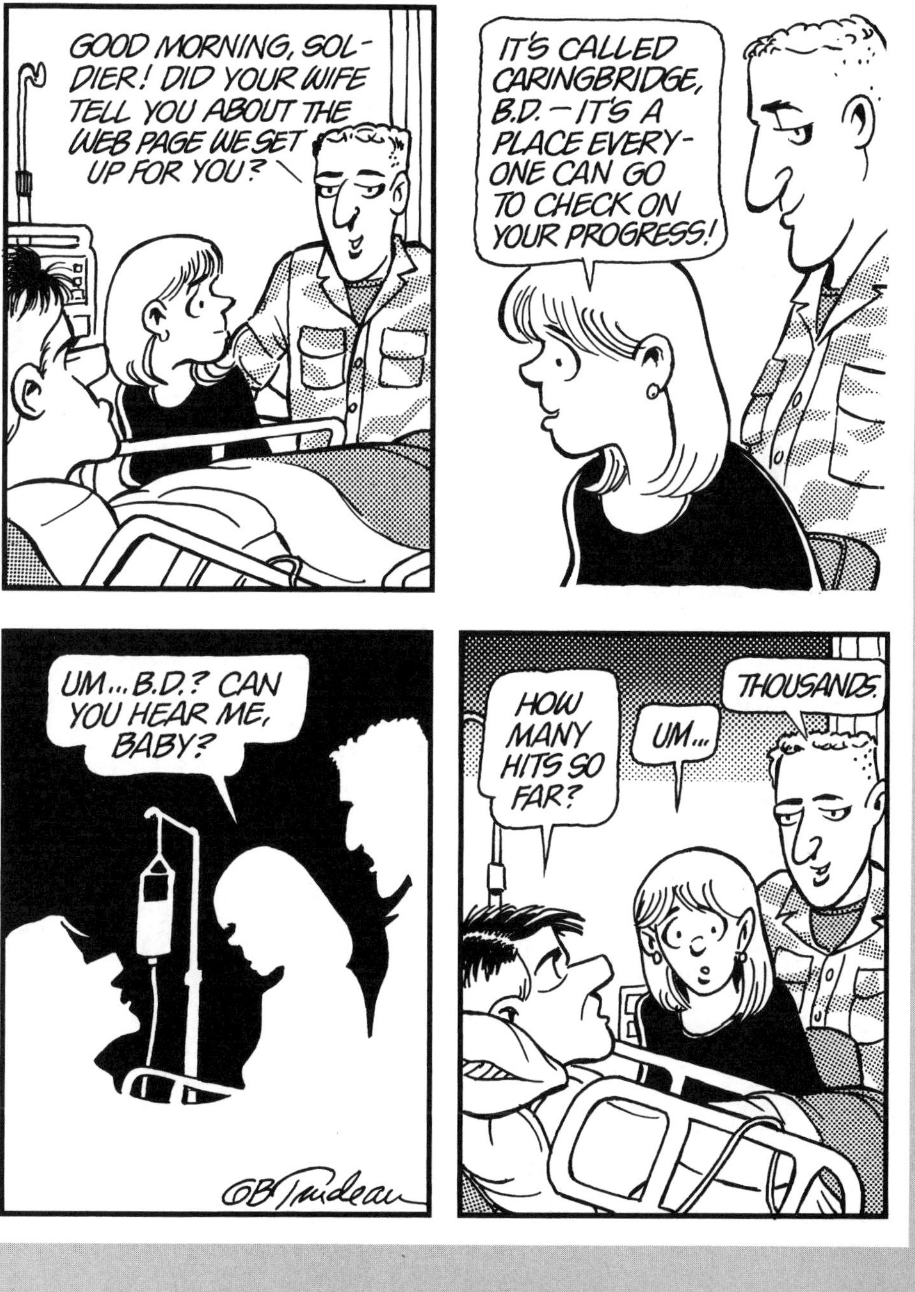
GOOD MORNING, SOLDIER! DID YOUR WIFE TELL YOU ABOUT THE WEB PAGE WE SET UP FOR YOU?
IT'S CALLED CARINGBRIDGE, B.D. — IT'S A PLACE EVERYONE CAN GO TO CHECK ON YOUR PROGRESS!
UM...B.D.? CAN YOU HEAR ME, BABY?
HOW MANY HITS SO FAR?
UM...
THOUSANDS.
©B. Trudeau

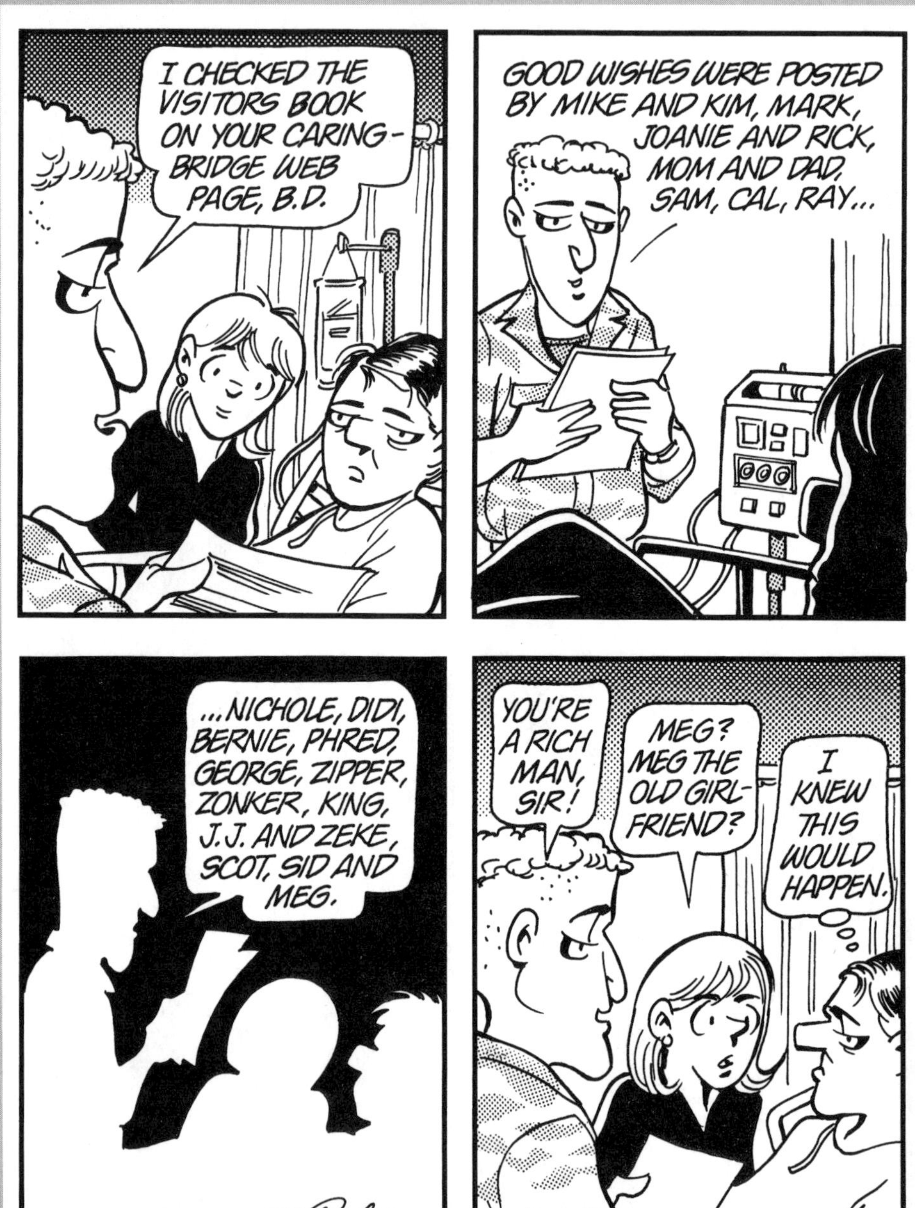
I CHECKED THE VISITORS BOOK ON YOUR CARING-BRIDGE WEB PAGE, B.D.
GOOD WISHES WERE POSTED BY MIKE AND KIM, MARK, JOANIE AND RICK, MOM AND DAD, SAM, CAL, RAY...
...NICHOLE, DIDI, BERNIE, PHRED, GEORGE, ZIPPER, ZONKER, KING, J.J. AND ZEKE, SCOT, SID AND MEG.
GB Trudeau
YOU'RE A RICH MAN, SIR!
MEG? MEG THE OLD GIRL-FRIEND?
I KNEW THIS WOULD HAPPEN.

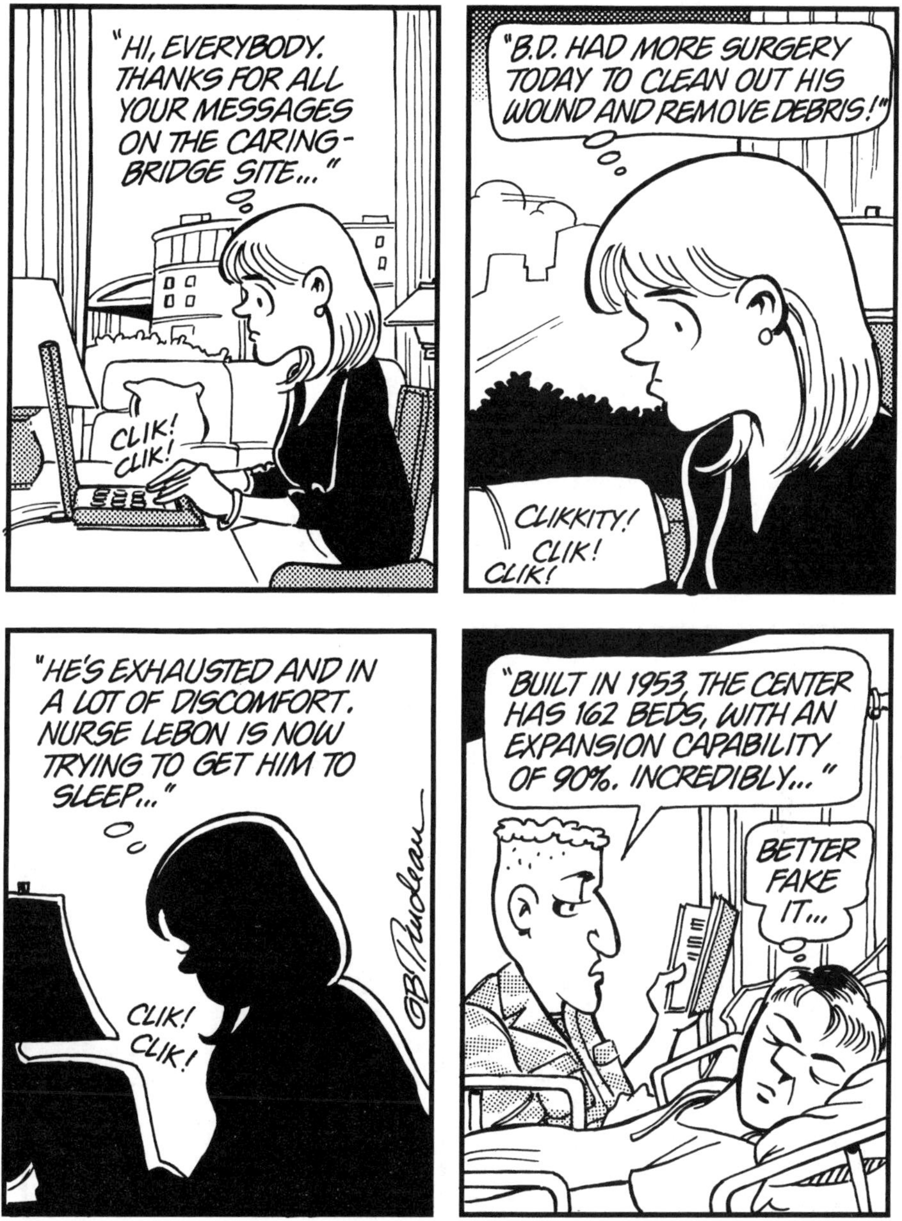
"HI, EVERYBODY. THANKS FOR ALL YOUR MESSAGES ON THE CARING-BRIDGE SITE..."
CLIK! CLIK!
"B.D. HAD MORE SURGERY TODAY TO CLEAN OUT HIS WOUND AND REMOVE DEBRIS!"
CLIKKITY! CLIK! CLIK!
"HE'S EXHAUSTED AND IN A LOT OF DISCOMFORT. NURSE LEBON IS NOW TRYING TO GET HIM TO SLEEP..."
CLIK! CLIK!
©B Trudeau
"BUILT IN 1953, THE CENTER HAS 162 BEDS, WITH AN EXPANSION CAPABILITY OF 90%. INCREDIBLY..."
BETTER FAKE IT...

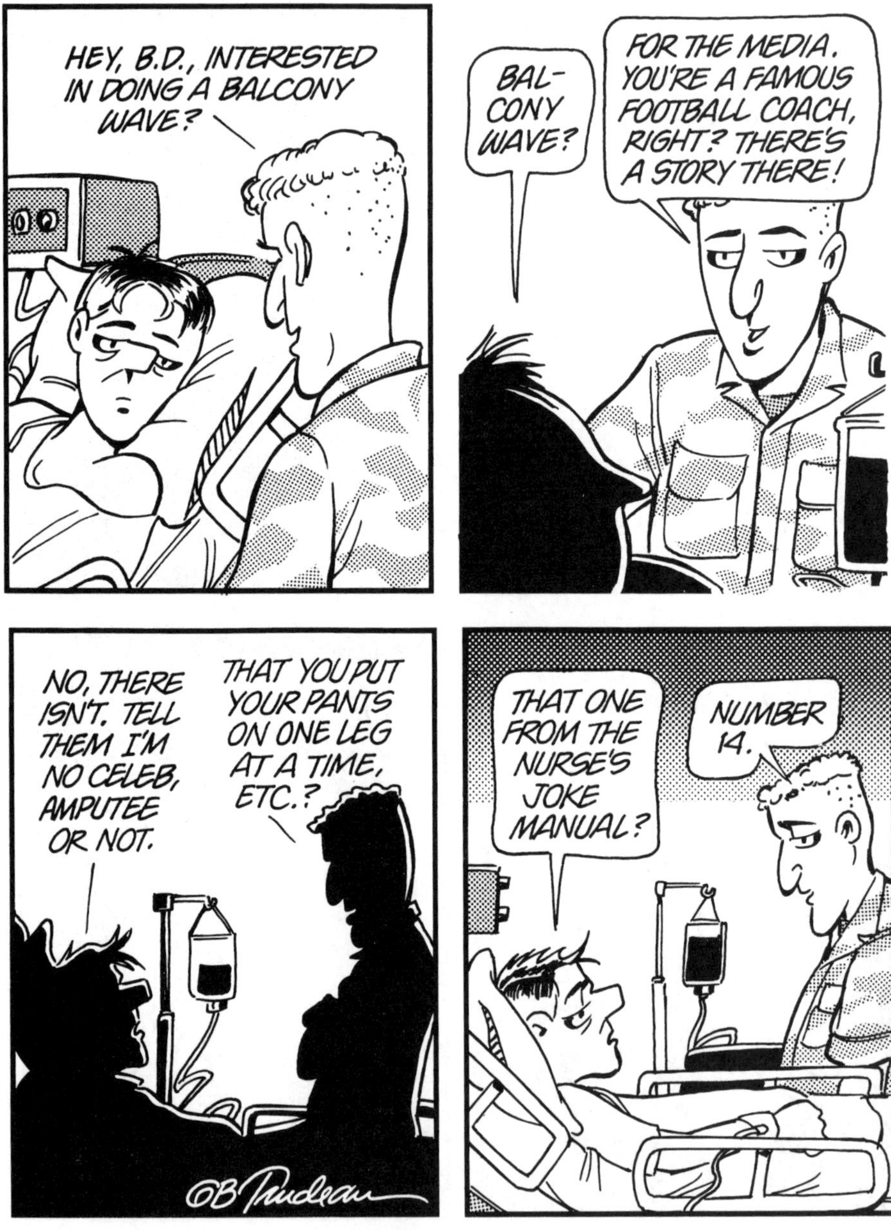
HEY, B.D., INTERESTED IN DOING A BALCONY WAVE?
BAL-CONY WAVE?
FOR THE MEDIA. YOU'RE A FAMOUS FOOTBALL COACH, RIGHT? THERE'S A STORY THERE!
NO, THERE ISN'T. TELL THEM I'M NO CELEB, AMPUTEE OR NOT.
THAT YOU PUT YOUR PANTS ON ONE LEG AT A TIME, ETC.?
THAT ONE FROM THE NURSE'S JOKE MANUAL?
NUMBER 14.
©B Trudeau

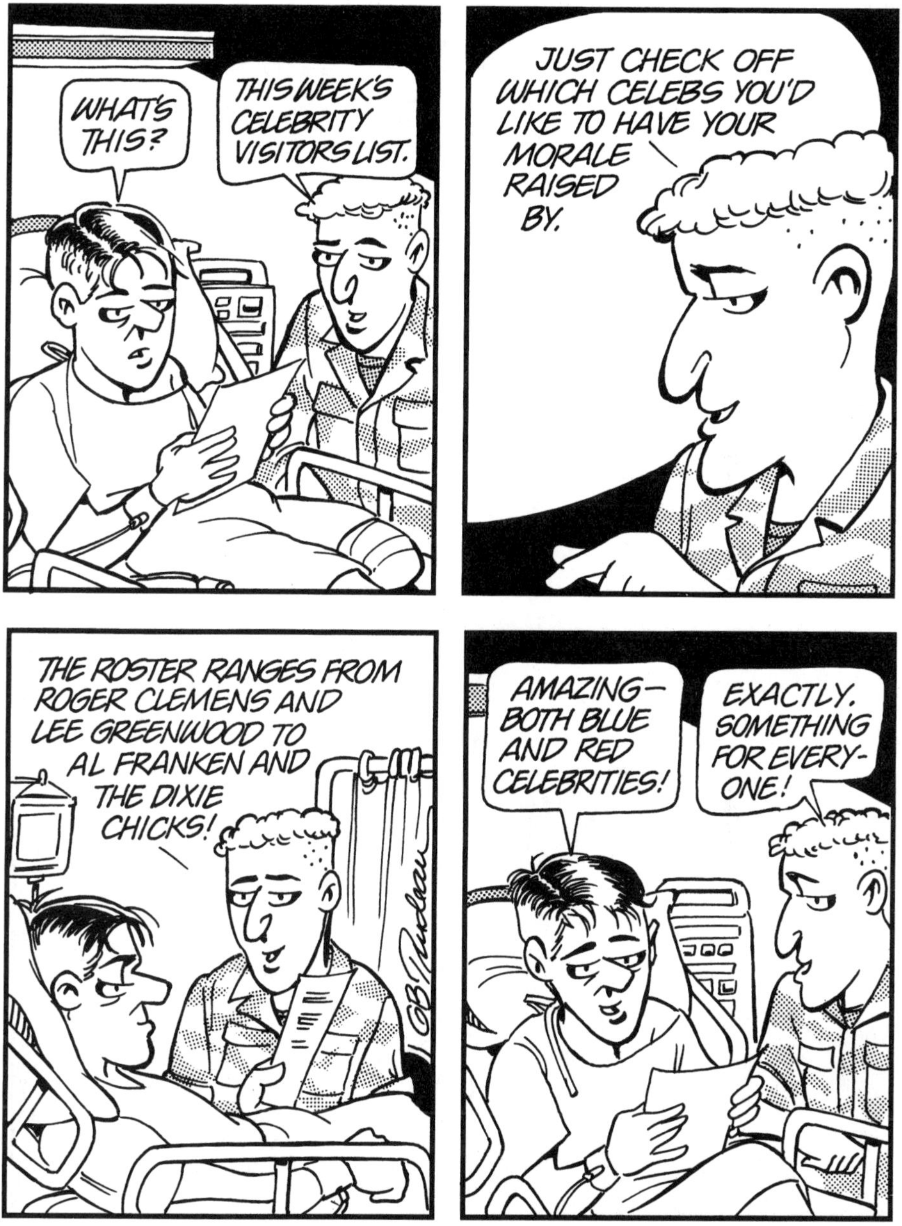
WHAT'S THIS?
THIS WEEK'S CELEBRITY VISITORS LIST.
JUST CHECK OFF WHICH CELEBS YOU'D LIKE TO HAVE YOUR MORALE RAISED BY.
THE ROSTER RANGES FROM ROGER CLEMENS AND LEE GREENWOOD TO AL FRANKEN AND THE DIXIE CHICKS!
AMAZING— BOTH BLUE AND RED CELEBRITIES!
EXACTLY. SOMETHING FOR EVERY-ONE!

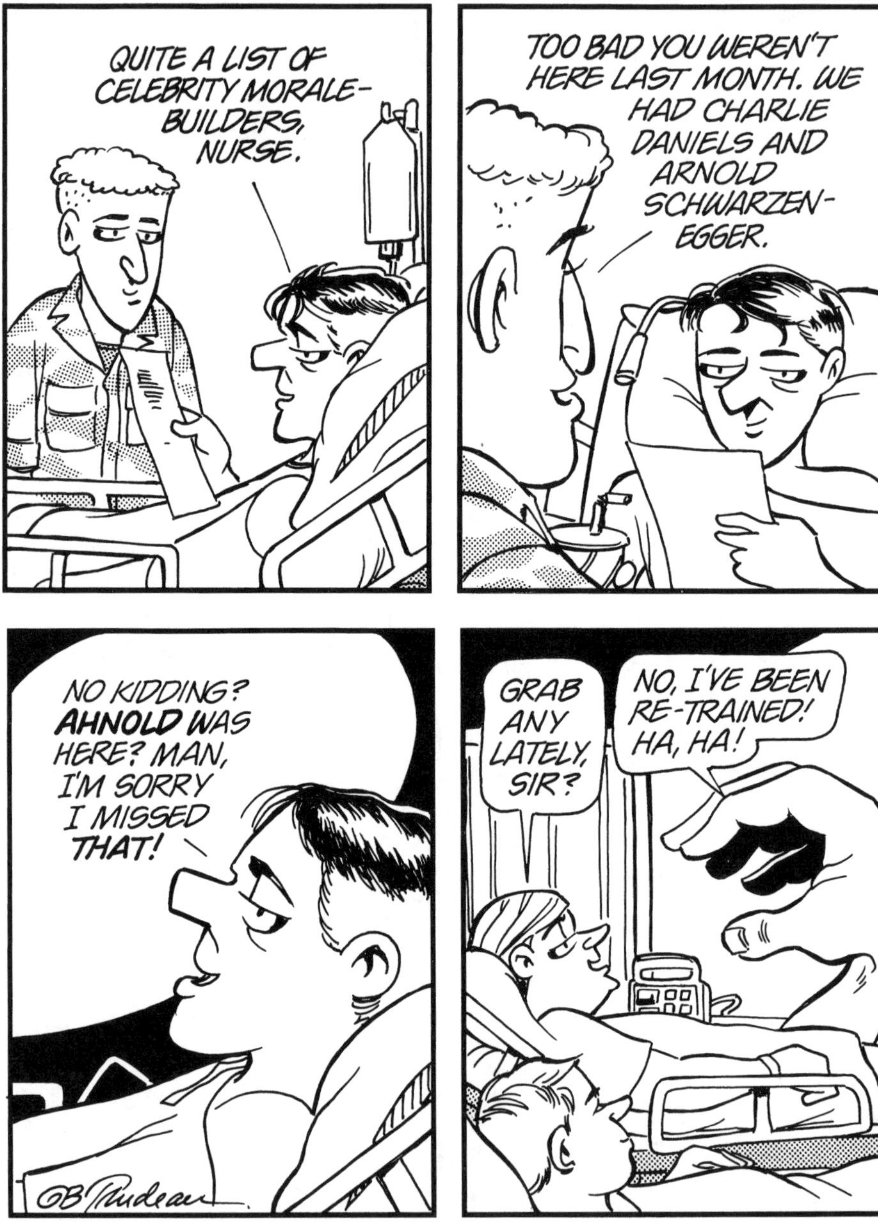
QUITE A LIST OF CELEBRITY MORALE-BUILDERS, NURSE.
TOO BAD YOU WEREN'T HERE LAST MONTH. WE HAD CHARLIE DANIELS AND ARNOLD SCHWARZEN-EGGER.
NO KIDDING? **AHNOLD** WAS HERE? MAN, I'M SORRY I MISSED **THAT**!
GRAB ANY LATELY, SIR?
NO, I'VE BEEN RE-TRAINED! HA, HA!
GB Trudeau

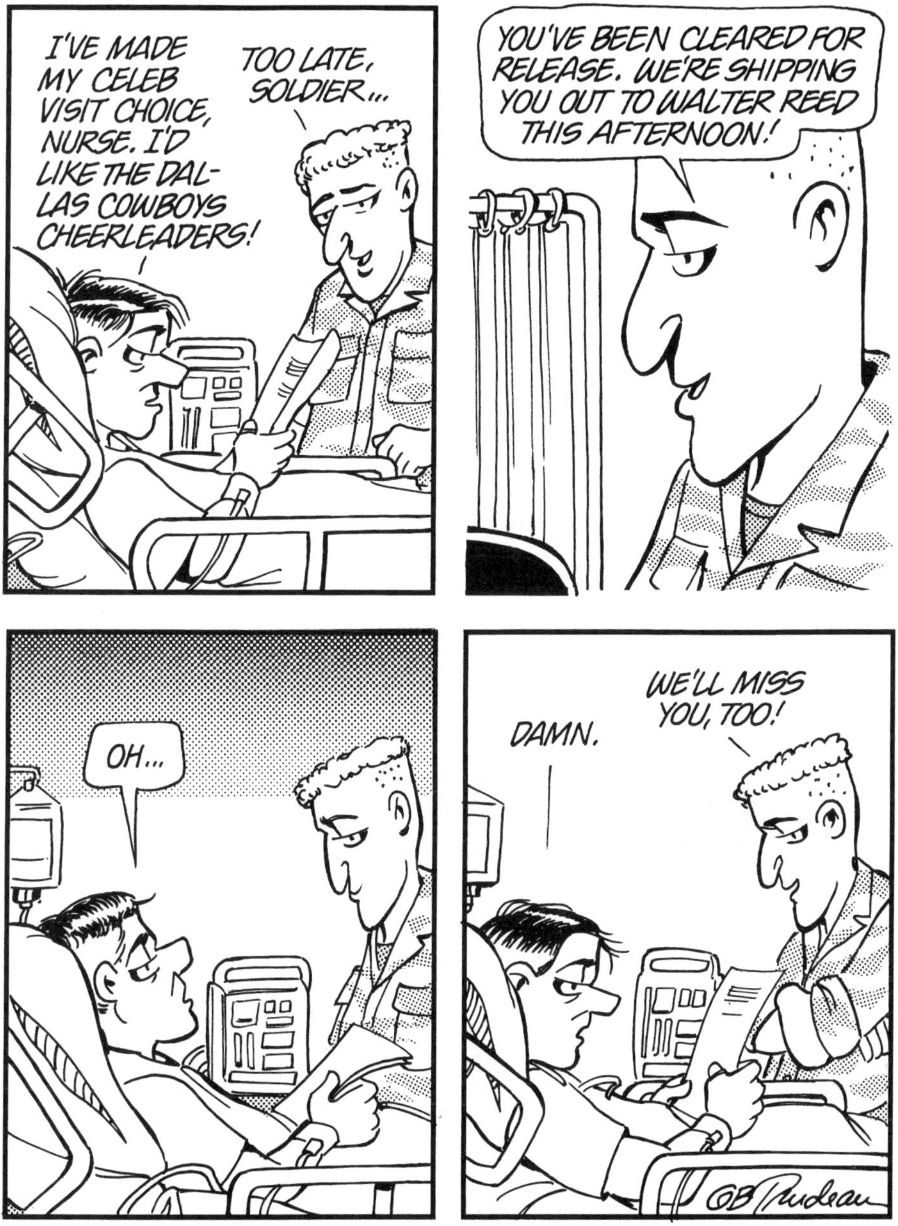
I'VE MADE MY CELEB VISIT CHOICE, NURSE. I'D LIKE THE DALLAS COWBOYS CHEERLEADERS!
TOO LATE, SOLDIER...
YOU'VE BEEN CLEARED FOR RELEASE. WE'RE SHIPPING YOU OUT TO WALTER REED THIS AFTERNOON!
OH...
DAMN.
WE'LL MISS YOU, TOO!
GB Trudeau

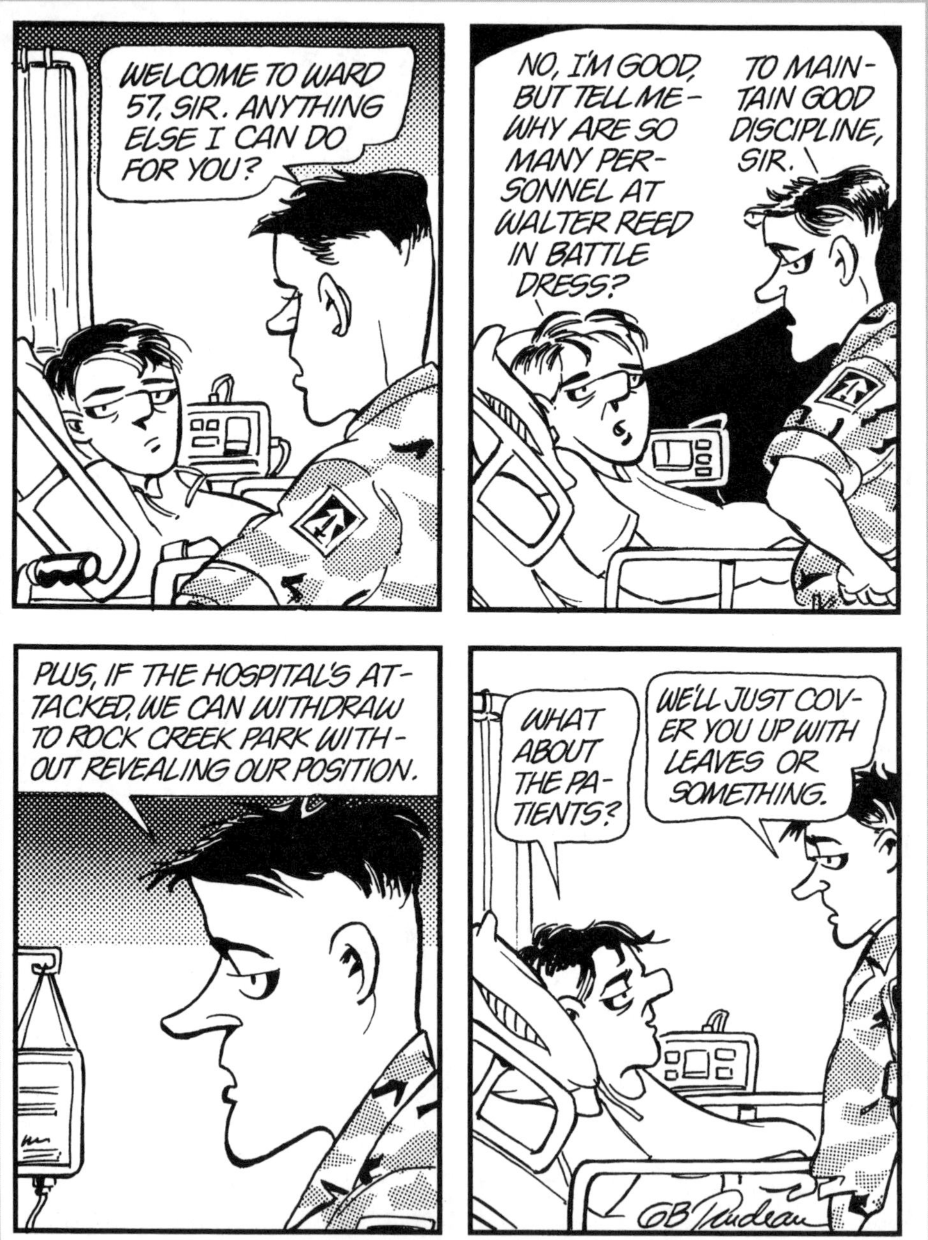
WELCOME TO WARD 57, SIR. ANYTHING ELSE I CAN DO FOR YOU?
NO, I'M GOOD, BUT TELL ME- WHY ARE SO MANY PERSONNEL AT WALTER REED IN BATTLE DRESS?
TO MAINTAIN GOOD DISCIPLINE, SIR.
PLUS, IF THE HOSPITAL'S ATTACKED, WE CAN WITHDRAW TO ROCK CREEK PARK WITHOUT REVEALING OUR POSITION.
WHAT ABOUT THE PATIENTS?
WE'LL JUST COVER YOU UP WITH LEAVES OR SOMETHING.
GB Trudeau

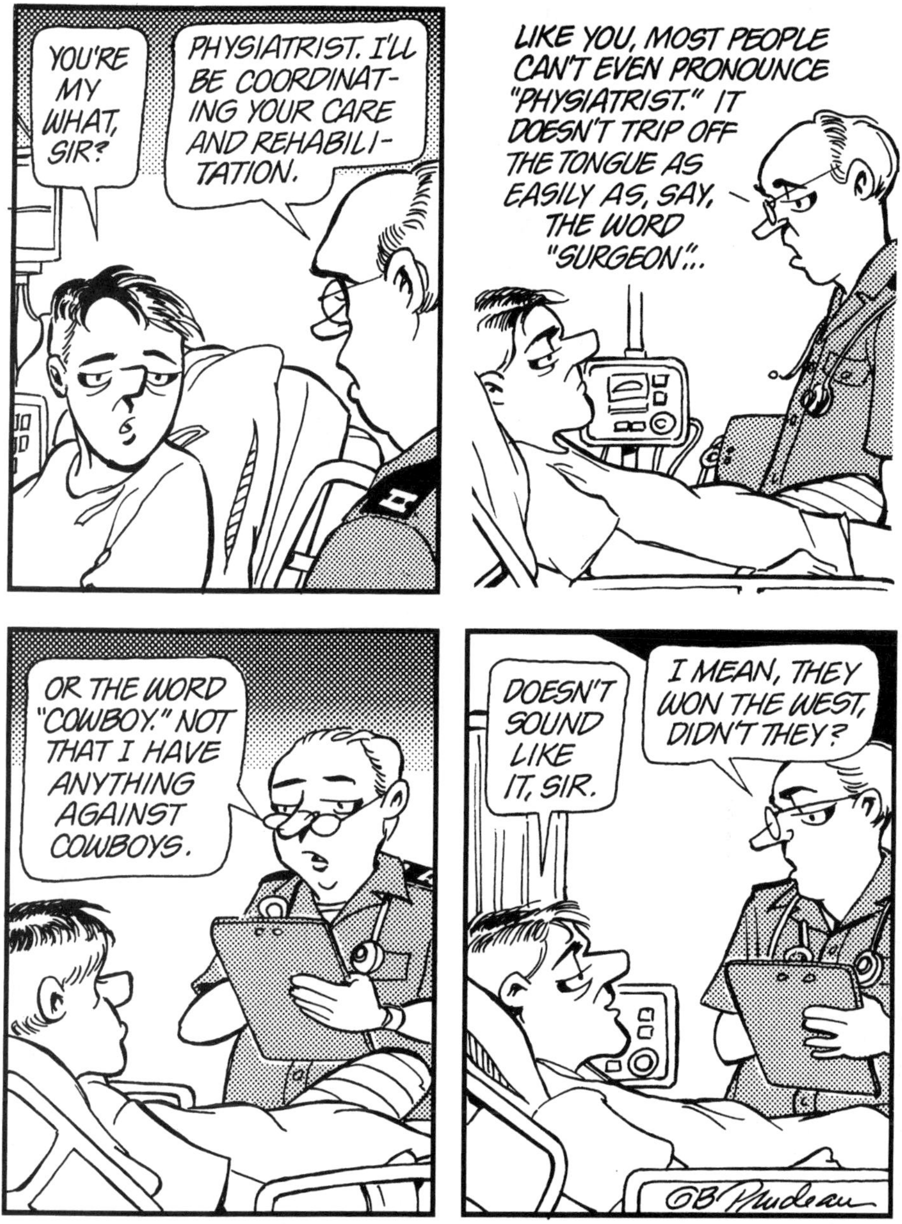

YOU'RE MY WHAT, SIR?
PHYSIATRIST. I'LL BE COORDINATING YOUR CARE AND REHABILITATION.
LIKE YOU, MOST PEOPLE CAN'T EVEN PRONOUNCE "PHYSIATRIST." IT DOESN'T TRIP OFF THE TONGUE AS EASILY AS, SAY, THE WORD "SURGEON"...
OR THE WORD "COWBOY." NOT THAT I HAVE ANYTHING AGAINST COWBOYS.
DOESN'T SOUND LIKE IT, SIR.
I MEAN, THEY WON THE WEST, DIDN'T THEY?
©B Trudeau

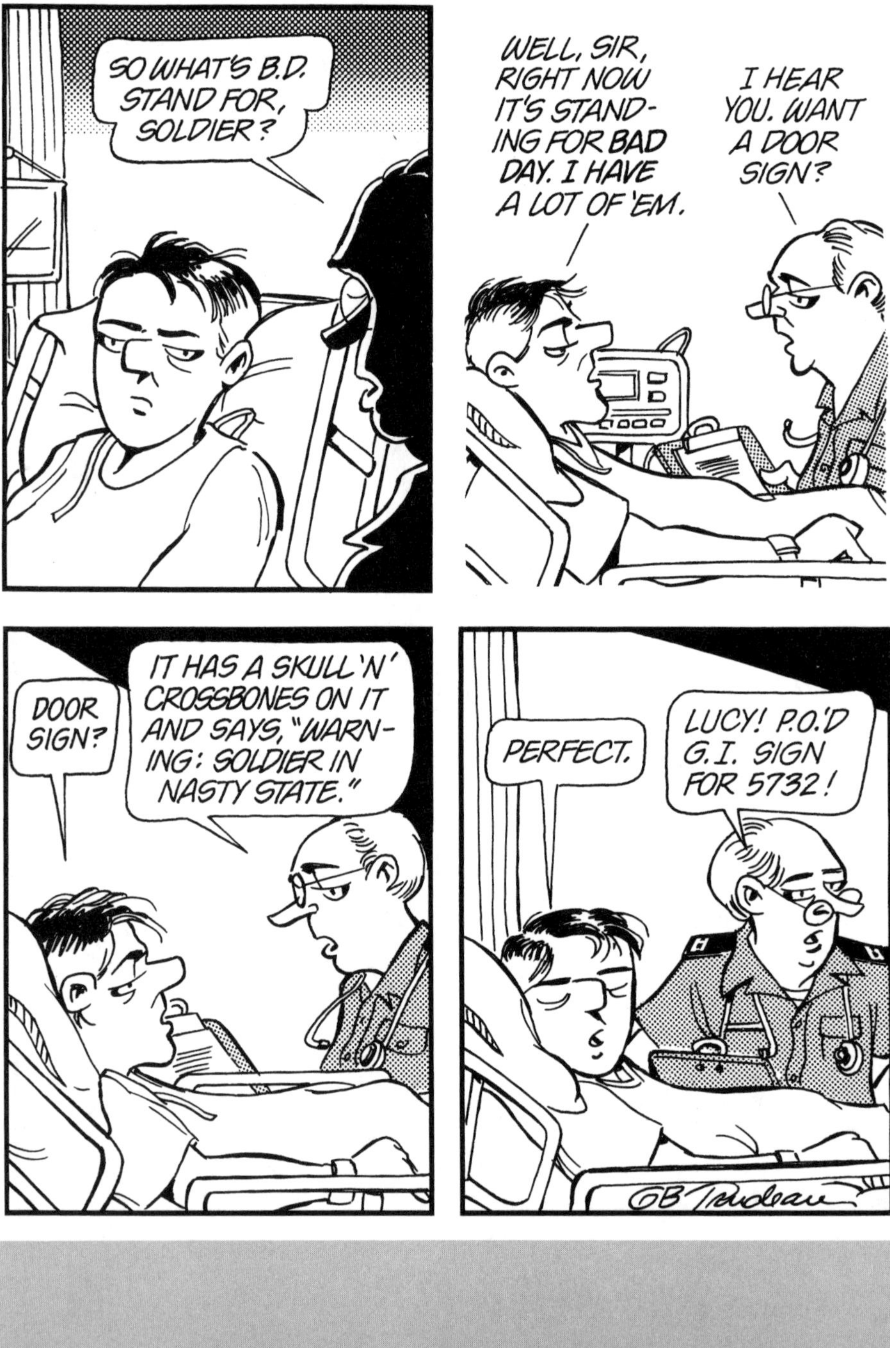
SO WHAT'S B.D. STAND FOR, SOLDIER?
WELL, SIR, RIGHT NOW IT'S STANDING FOR BAD DAY. I HAVE A LOT OF 'EM.
I HEAR YOU. WANT A DOOR SIGN?
DOOR SIGN?
IT HAS A SKULL 'N' CROSSBONES ON IT AND SAYS, "WARNING: SOLDIER IN NASTY STATE."
PERFECT.
LUCY! P.O.'D G.I. SIGN FOR 5732!
GB Trudeau

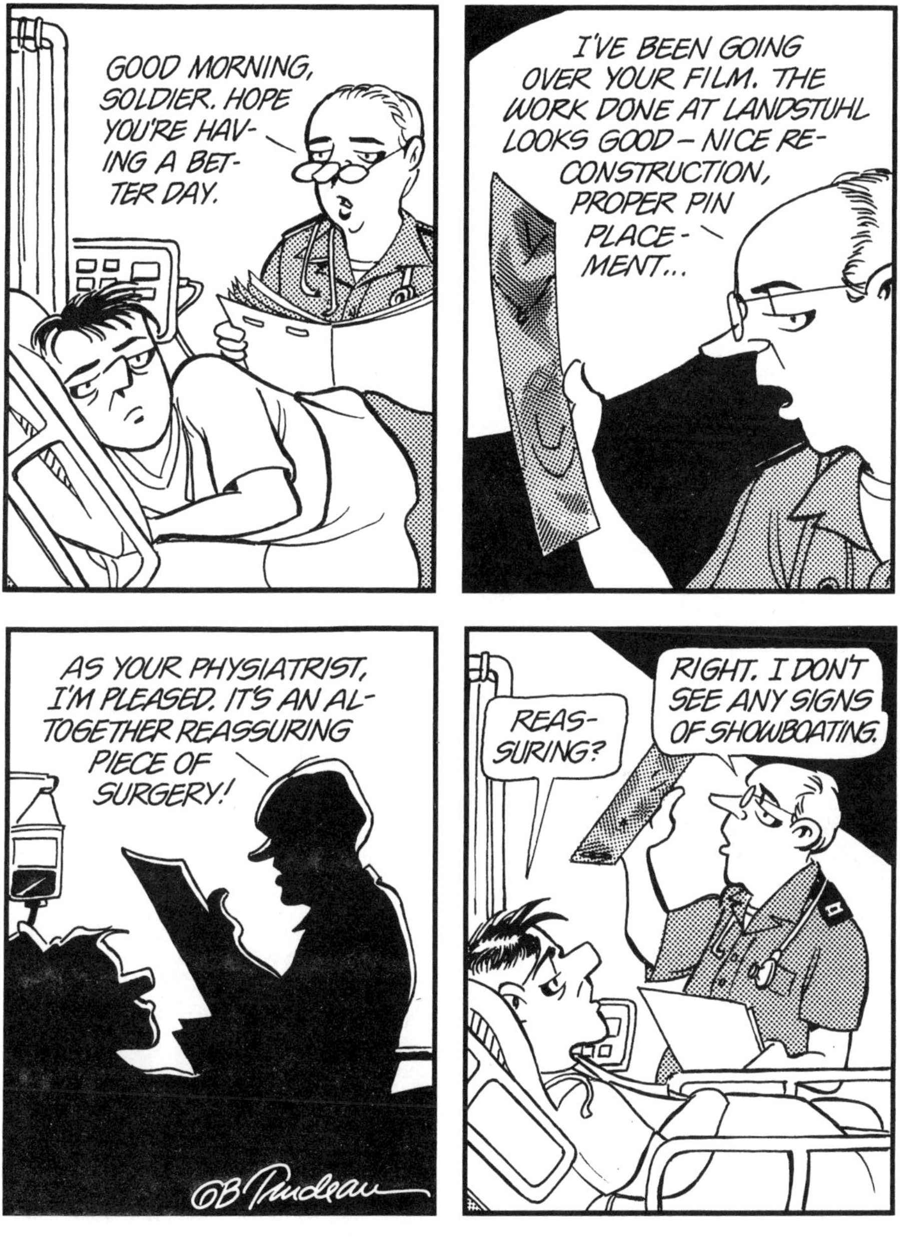
GOOD MORNING, SOLDIER. HOPE YOU'RE HAVING A BETTER DAY.
I'VE BEEN GOING OVER YOUR FILM. THE WORK DONE AT LANDSTUHL LOOKS GOOD – NICE RECONSTRUCTION, PROPER PIN PLACEMENT...
AS YOUR PHYSIATRIST, I'M PLEASED. IT'S AN ALTOGETHER REASSURING PIECE OF SURGERY!
REASSURING?
RIGHT. I DON'T SEE ANY SIGNS OF SHOWBOATING.
©B Trudeau

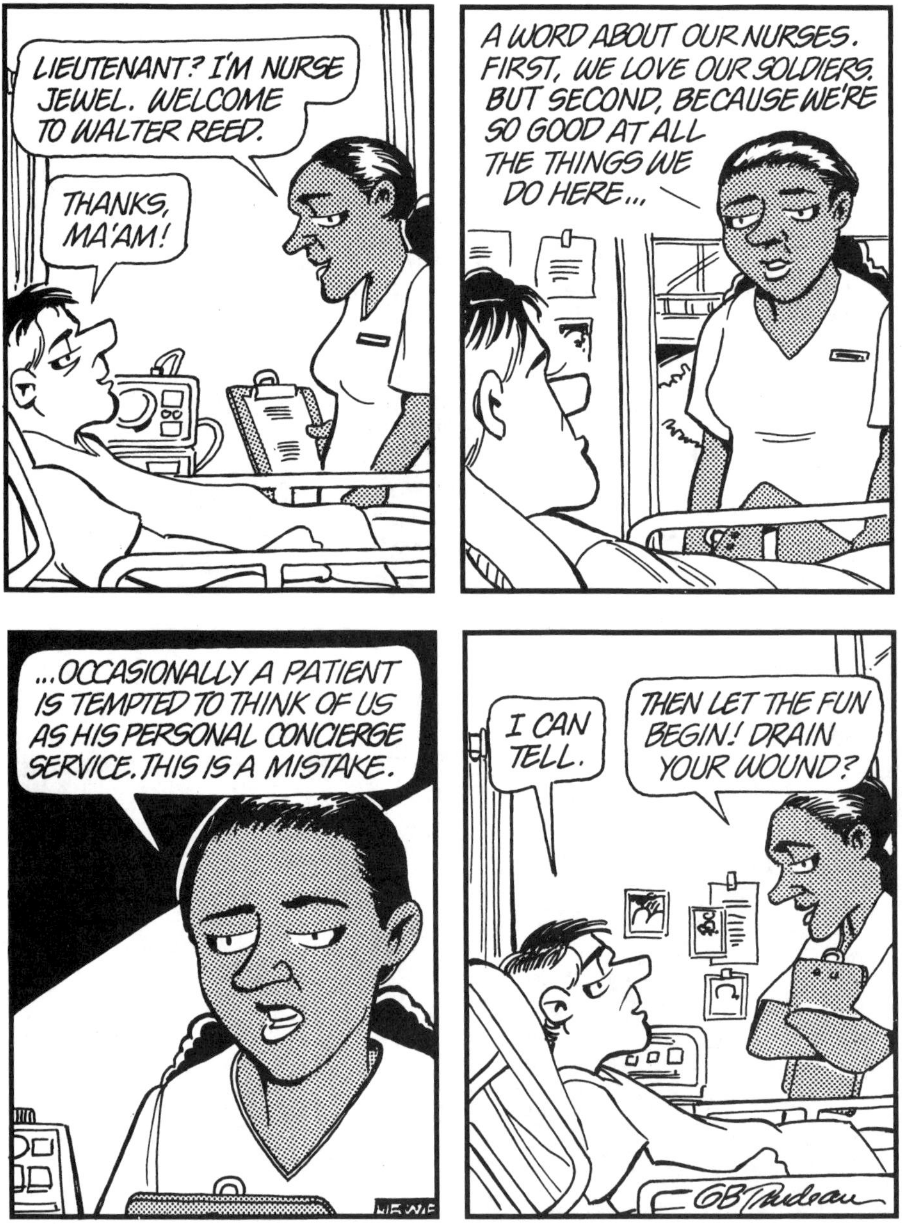
LIEUTENANT? I'M NURSE JEWEL. WELCOME TO WALTER REED.
THANKS, MA'AM!
A WORD ABOUT OUR NURSES. FIRST, WE LOVE OUR SOLDIERS. BUT SECOND, BECAUSE WE'RE SO GOOD AT ALL THE THINGS WE DO HERE...
...OCCASIONALLY A PATIENT IS TEMPTED TO THINK OF US AS HIS PERSONAL CONCIERGE SERVICE. THIS IS A MISTAKE.
I CAN TELL.
THEN LET THE FUN BEGIN! DRAIN YOUR WOUND?
GBTrudeau

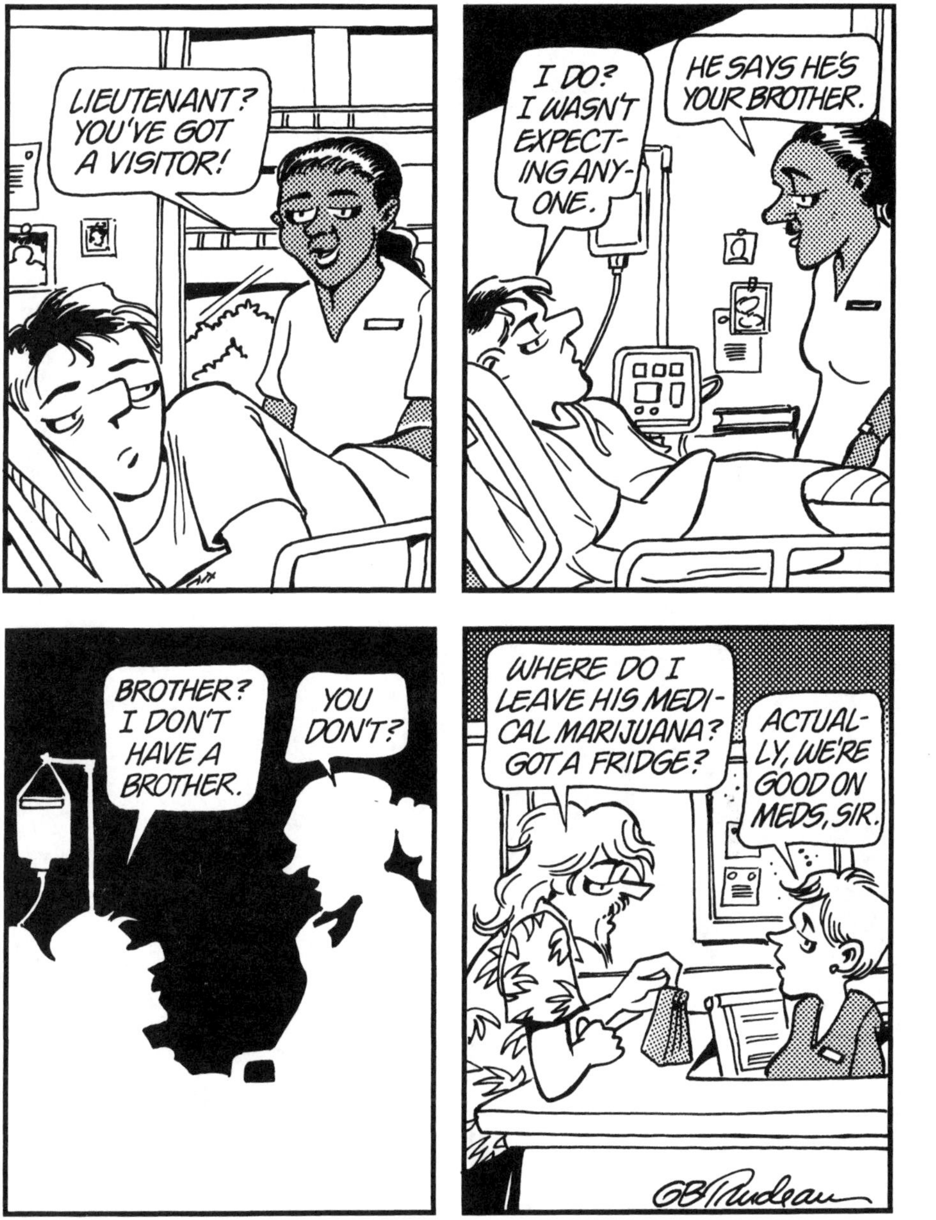
LIEUTENANT? YOU'VE GOT A VISITOR!
I DO? I WASN'T EXPECTING ANYONE.
HE SAYS HE'S YOUR BROTHER.
BROTHER? I DON'T HAVE A BROTHER.
YOU DON'T?
WHERE DO I LEAVE HIS MEDICAL MARIJUANA? GOT A FRIDGE?
ACTUALLY, WE'RE GOOD ON MEDS, SIR.
GBTrudeau

WHY ARE YOU LOOKING AT ME LIKE THAT, MA'AM?
BEFORE YOUR GUEST COMES IN, I NEED TO SEE YOU SIT UP TODAY...
YOU'RE A TYRANT, MA'AM. I TOLD YOU I CAN'T DO IT YET...
YES, YOU CAN. JUST MOVE VERY SLOWLY.
MAYBE IF I TWIST AROUND THIS WAY...
NO! DON'T...
I KNOW THAT SCREAM.
I WONDER IF ANYONE TOLD HIM ABOUT HIS SKIN GRAFT.
GBTrudeau

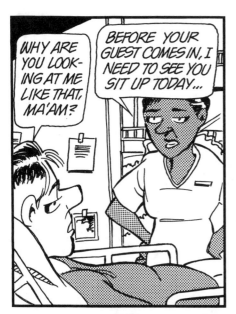

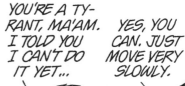

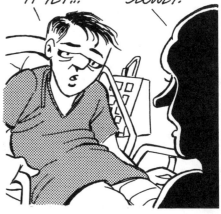

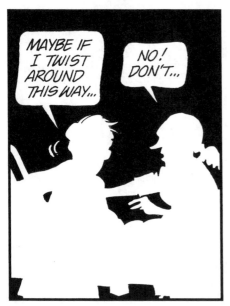

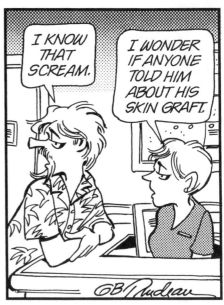

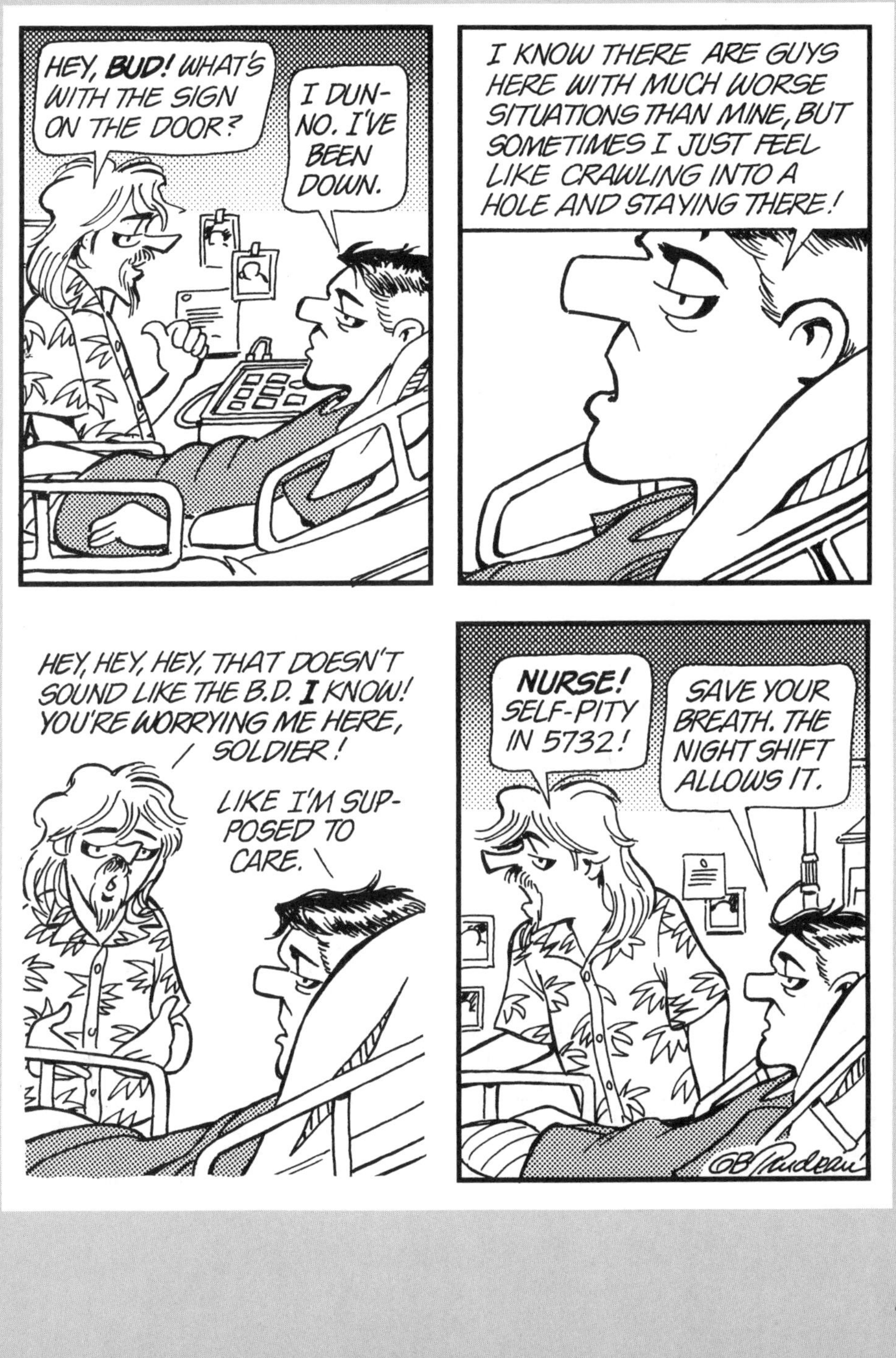

HEY, **BUD!** WHAT'S WITH THE SIGN ON THE DOOR?
I DUN-NO. I'VE BEEN DOWN.
I KNOW THERE ARE GUYS HERE WITH MUCH WORSE SITUATIONS THAN MINE, BUT SOMETIMES I JUST FEEL LIKE CRAWLING INTO A HOLE AND STAYING THERE!
HEY, HEY, HEY, THAT DOESN'T SOUND LIKE THE B.D. **I** KNOW! YOU'RE WORRYING ME HERE, SOLDIER!
LIKE I'M SUP-POSED TO CARE.
NURSE! SELF-PITY IN 5732!
SAVE YOUR BREATH. THE NIGHT SHIFT ALLOWS IT.
GB Trudeau

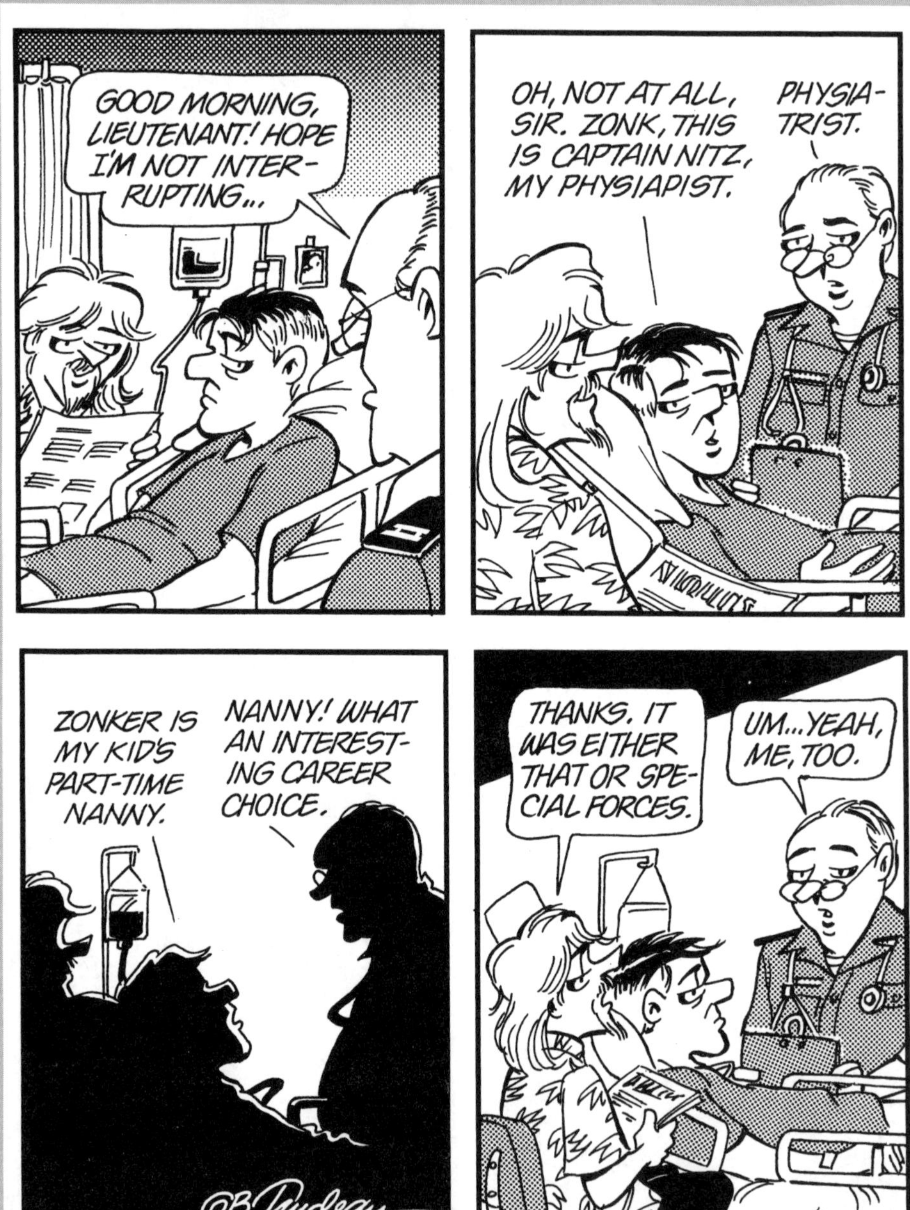
GOOD MORNING, LIEUTENANT! HOPE I'M NOT INTERRUPTING...
OH, NOT AT ALL, SIR. ZONK, THIS IS CAPTAIN NITZ, MY PHYSIAPIST.
PHYSIATRIST.
ZONKER IS MY KID'S PART-TIME NANNY.
NANNY! WHAT AN INTERESTING CAREER CHOICE.
©B Trudeau
THANKS. IT WAS EITHER THAT OR SPECIAL FORCES.
UM... YEAH, ME, TOO.

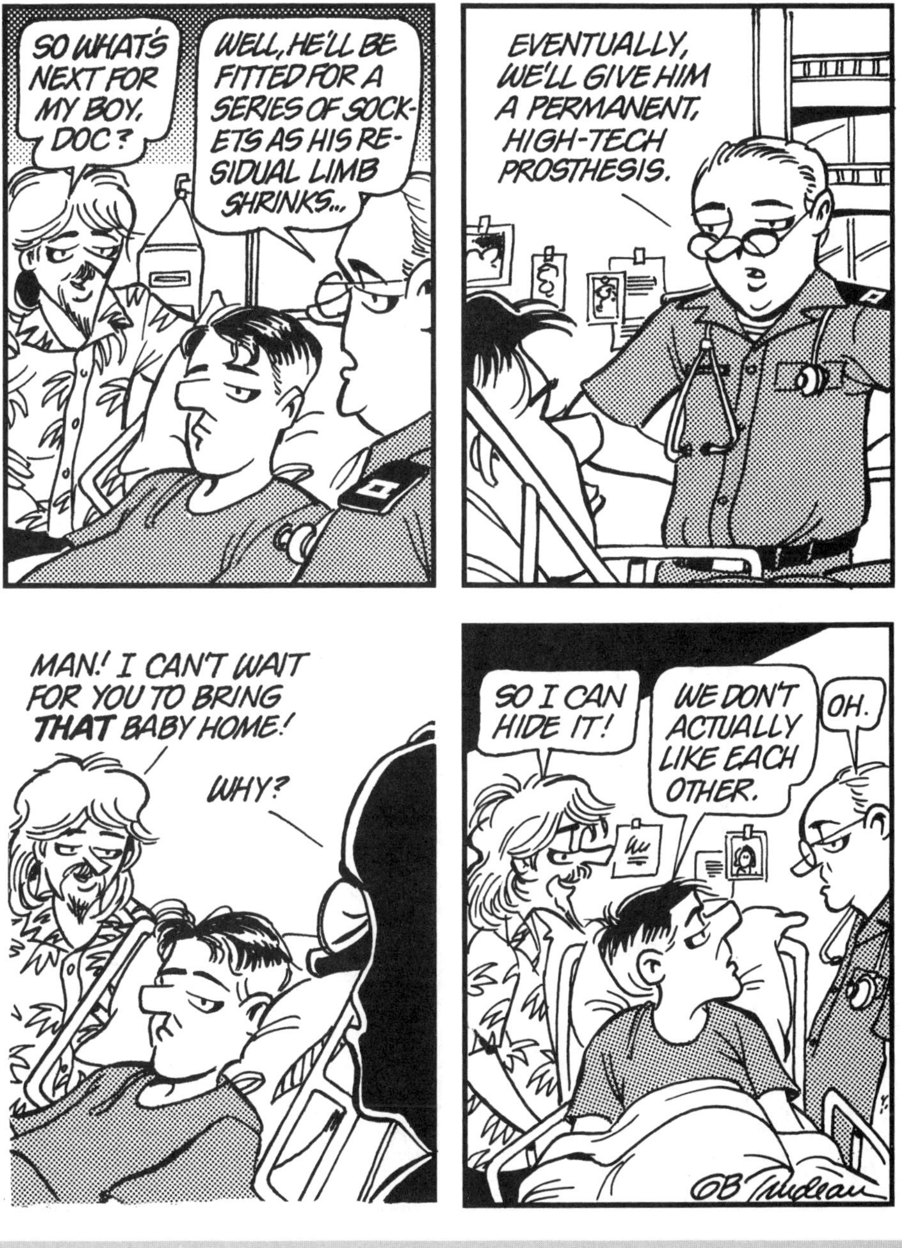

SO WHAT'S NEXT FOR MY BOY, DOC?
WELL, HE'LL BE FITTED FOR A SERIES OF SOCK-ETS AS HIS RE-SIDUAL LIMB SHRINKS...
EVENTUALLY, WE'LL GIVE HIM A PERMANENT, HIGH-TECH PROSTHESIS.
MAN! I CAN'T WAIT FOR YOU TO BRING **THAT** BABY HOME!
WHY?
SO I CAN HIDE IT!
WE DON'T ACTUALLY LIKE EACH OTHER.
OH.
©B Trudeau

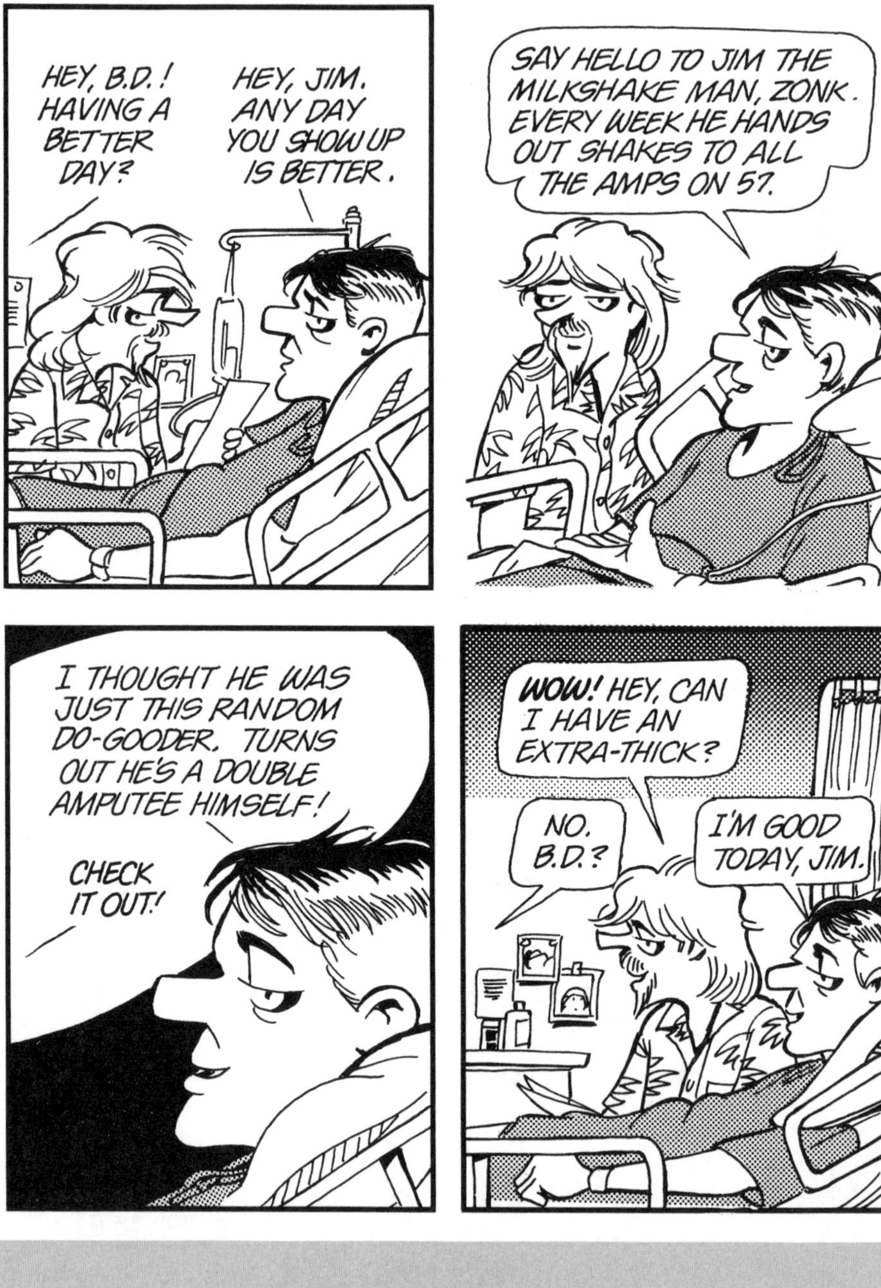
HEY, B.D.! HAVING A BETTER DAY?
HEY, JIM. ANY DAY YOU SHOW UP IS BETTER.
SAY HELLO TO JIM THE MILKSHAKE MAN, ZONK. EVERY WEEK HE HANDS OUT SHAKES TO ALL THE AMPS ON 57.
I THOUGHT HE WAS JUST THIS RANDOM DO-GOODER. TURNS OUT HE'S A DOUBLE AMPUTEE HIMSELF!
CHECK IT OUT!
WOW! HEY, CAN I HAVE AN EXTRA-THICK?
NO. B.D.?
I'M GOOD TODAY, JIM.

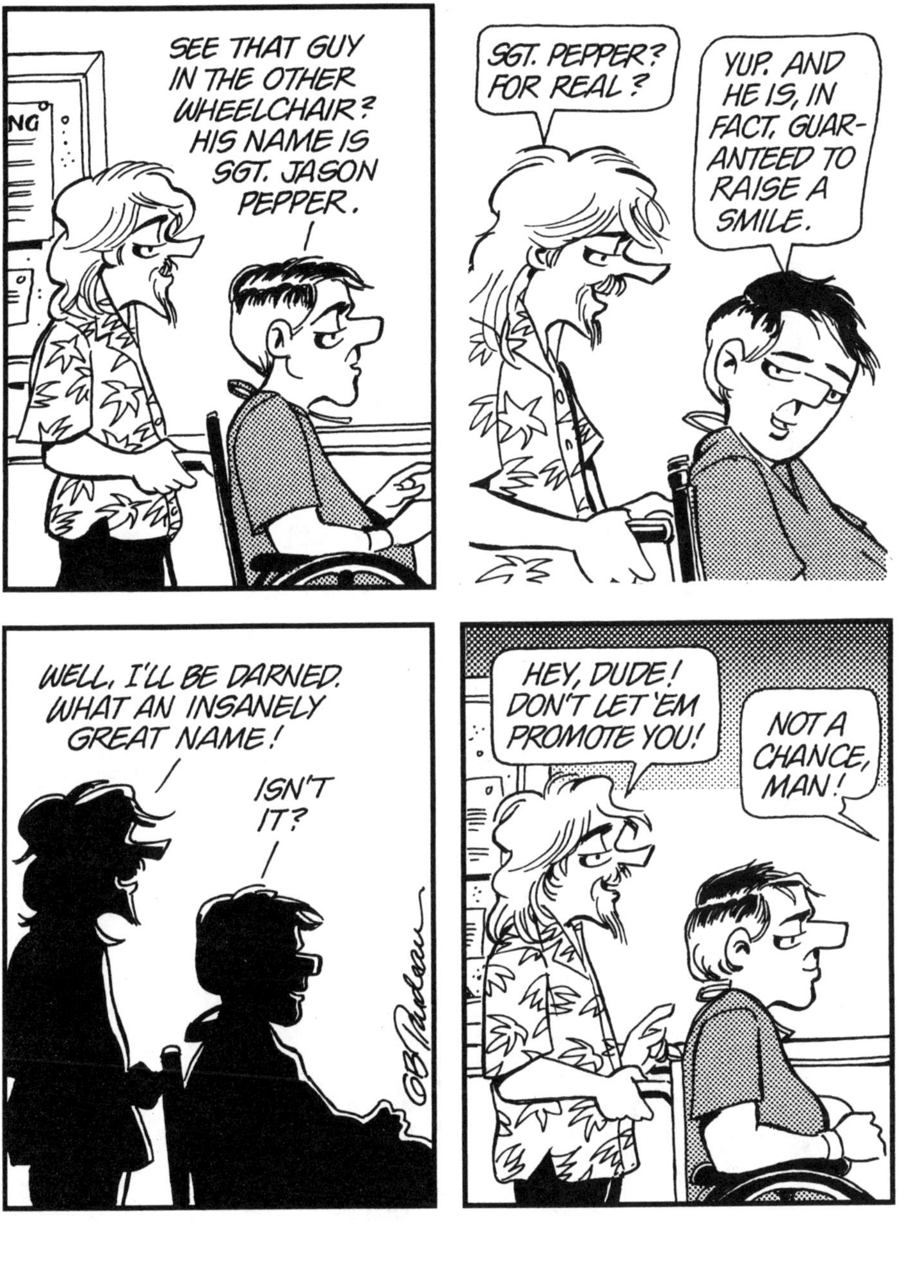

SEE THAT GUY IN THE OTHER WHEELCHAIR? HIS NAME IS SGT. JASON PEPPER.
SGT. PEPPER? FOR REAL?
YUP. AND HE IS, IN FACT, GUARANTEED TO RAISE A SMILE.
WELL, I'LL BE DARNED. WHAT AN INSANELY GREAT NAME!
ISN'T IT?
HEY, DUDE! DON'T LET 'EM PROMOTE YOU!
NOT A CHANCE, MAN!

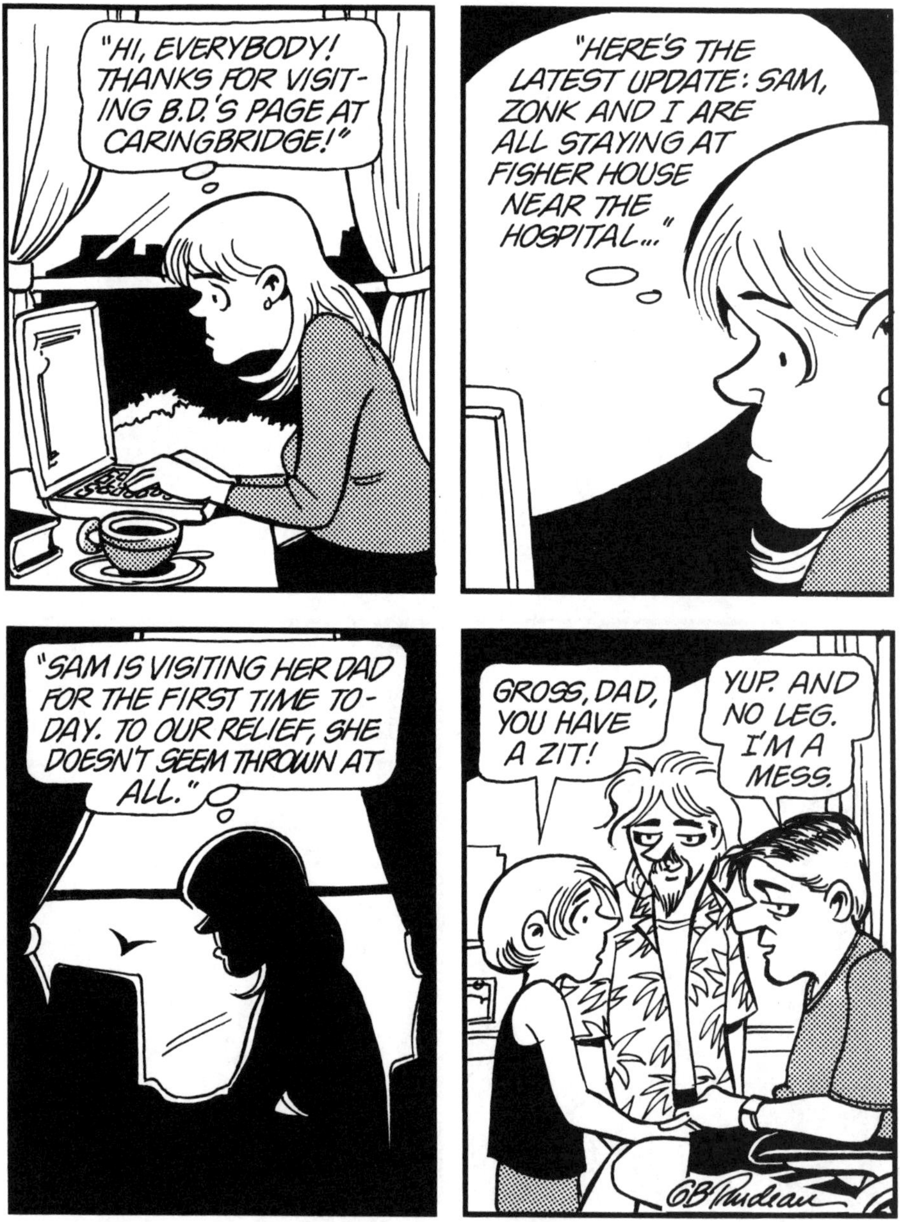
"HI, EVERYBODY! THANKS FOR VISIT-ING B.D.'S PAGE AT CARINGBRIDGE!"
"HERE'S THE LATEST UPDATE: SAM, ZONK AND I ARE ALL STAYING AT FISHER HOUSE NEAR THE HOSPITAL..."
"SAM IS VISITING HER DAD FOR THE FIRST TIME TO-DAY. TO OUR RELIEF, SHE DOESN'T SEEM THROWN AT ALL."
GROSS, DAD, YOU HAVE A ZIT!
YUP. AND NO LEG. I'M A MESS.
GBTrudeau

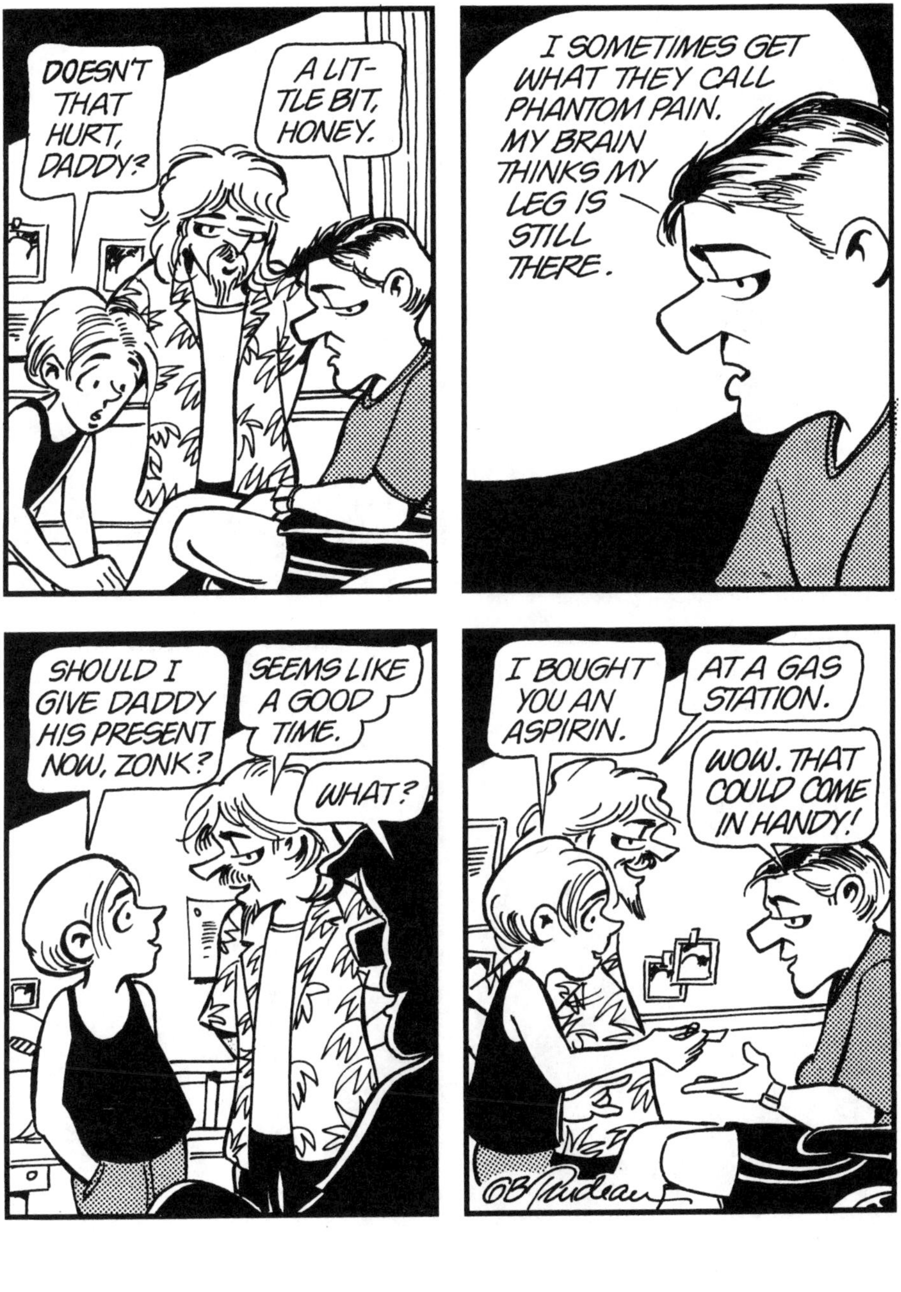
DOESN'T THAT HURT, DADDY?
A LITTLE BIT, HONEY.
I SOMETIMES GET WHAT THEY CALL PHANTOM PAIN. MY BRAIN THINKS MY LEG IS STILL THERE.
SHOULD I GIVE DADDY HIS PRESENT NOW, ZONK?
SEEMS LIKE A GOOD TIME.
WHAT?
I BOUGHT YOU AN ASPIRIN.
AT A GAS STATION.
WOW. THAT COULD COME IN HANDY!
©B Trudeau

I'VE BEEN REALLY WORRIED ABOUT YOU, DADDY.
I KNOW, HONEY. I'M SO SORRY.
AT FIRST I WAS JUST EXCITED YOU WERE COMING HOME, BUT THEN I JUST STARTED CRYING AND CRYING AND CRYING!
AND THEN I JUST STAYED IN MY ROOM AND WOULDN'T GO TO SCHOOL AND GOT MAD AT MOMMY AND WOULDN'T EAT!
BUT THEN ZONKER CALLED ME ON BEING A DRAMA QUEEN.
I MADE HER A LITTLE EMMY OUT OF FOAMBOARD.
GB Trudeau

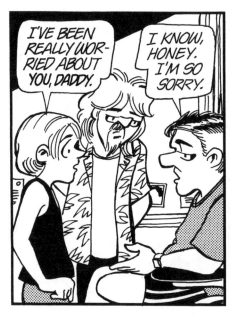

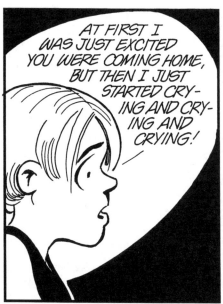

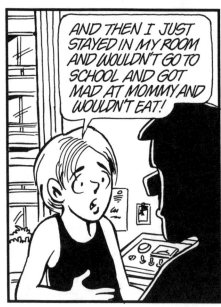

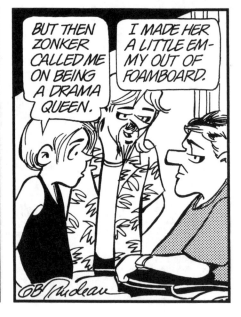

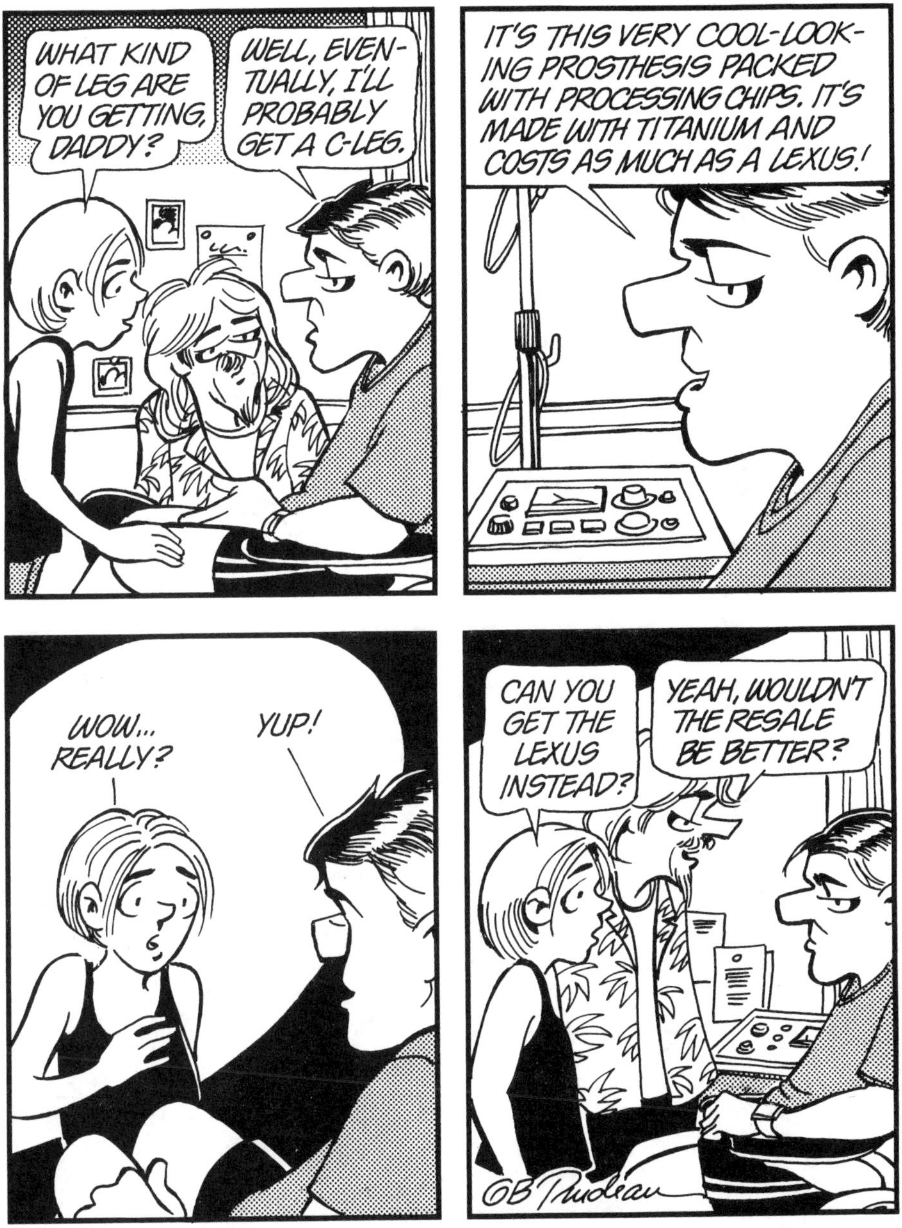
WHAT KIND OF LEG ARE YOU GETTING, DADDY?
WELL, EVENTUALLY, I'LL PROBABLY GET A C-LEG.
IT'S THIS VERY COOL-LOOKING PROSTHESIS PACKED WITH PROCESSING CHIPS. IT'S MADE WITH TITANIUM AND COSTS AS MUCH AS A LEXUS!
WOW... REALLY?
YUP!
CAN YOU GET THE LEXUS INSTEAD?
YEAH, WOULDN'T THE RESALE BE BETTER?
GB Trudeau

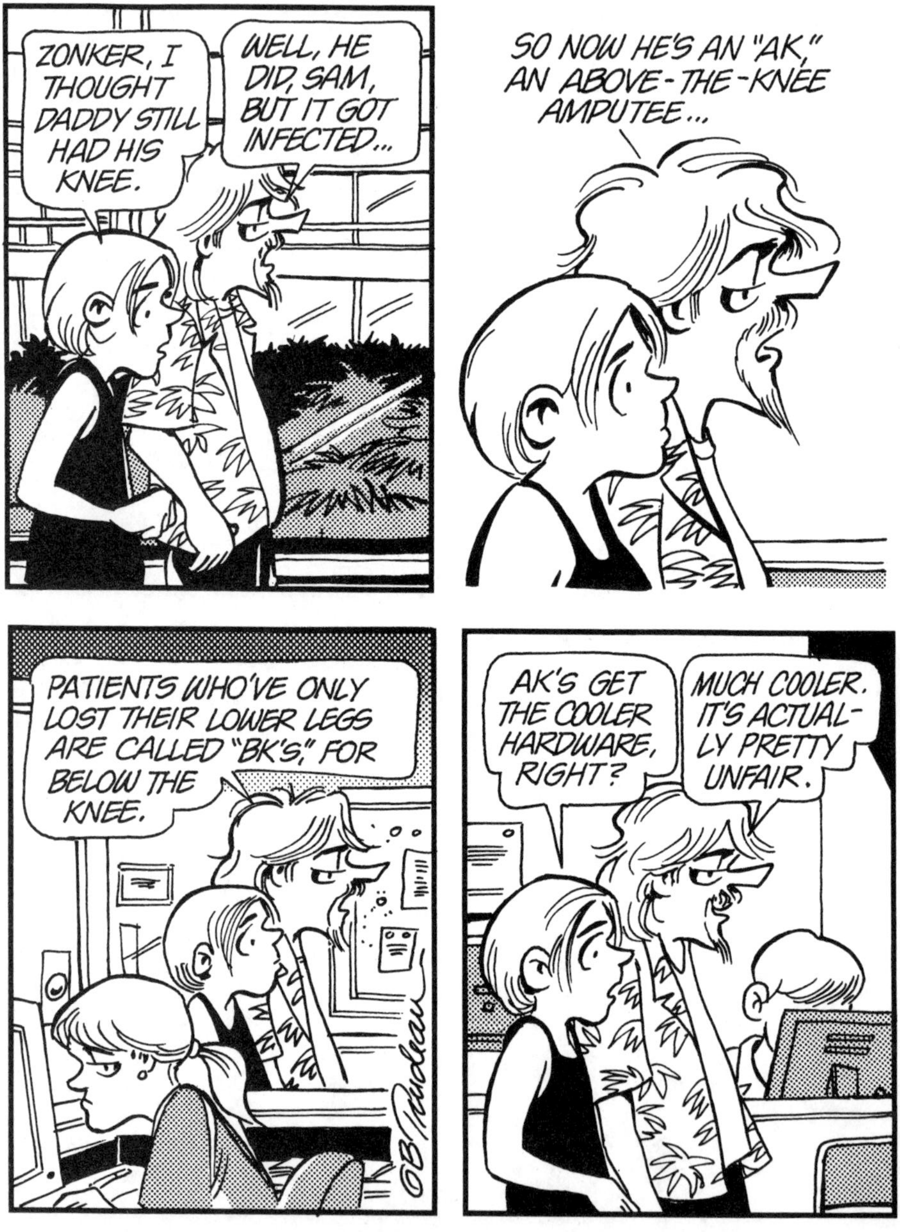
ZONKER, I THOUGHT DADDY STILL HAD HIS KNEE.
WELL, HE DID, SAM, BUT IT GOT INFECTED...
SO NOW HE'S AN "AK," AN ABOVE-THE-KNEE AMPUTEE...
PATIENTS WHO'VE ONLY LOST THEIR LOWER LEGS ARE CALLED "BK'S," FOR BELOW THE KNEE.
©B. Trudeau
AK'S GET THE COOLER HARDWARE, RIGHT?
MUCH COOLER. IT'S ACTUALLY PRETTY UNFAIR.

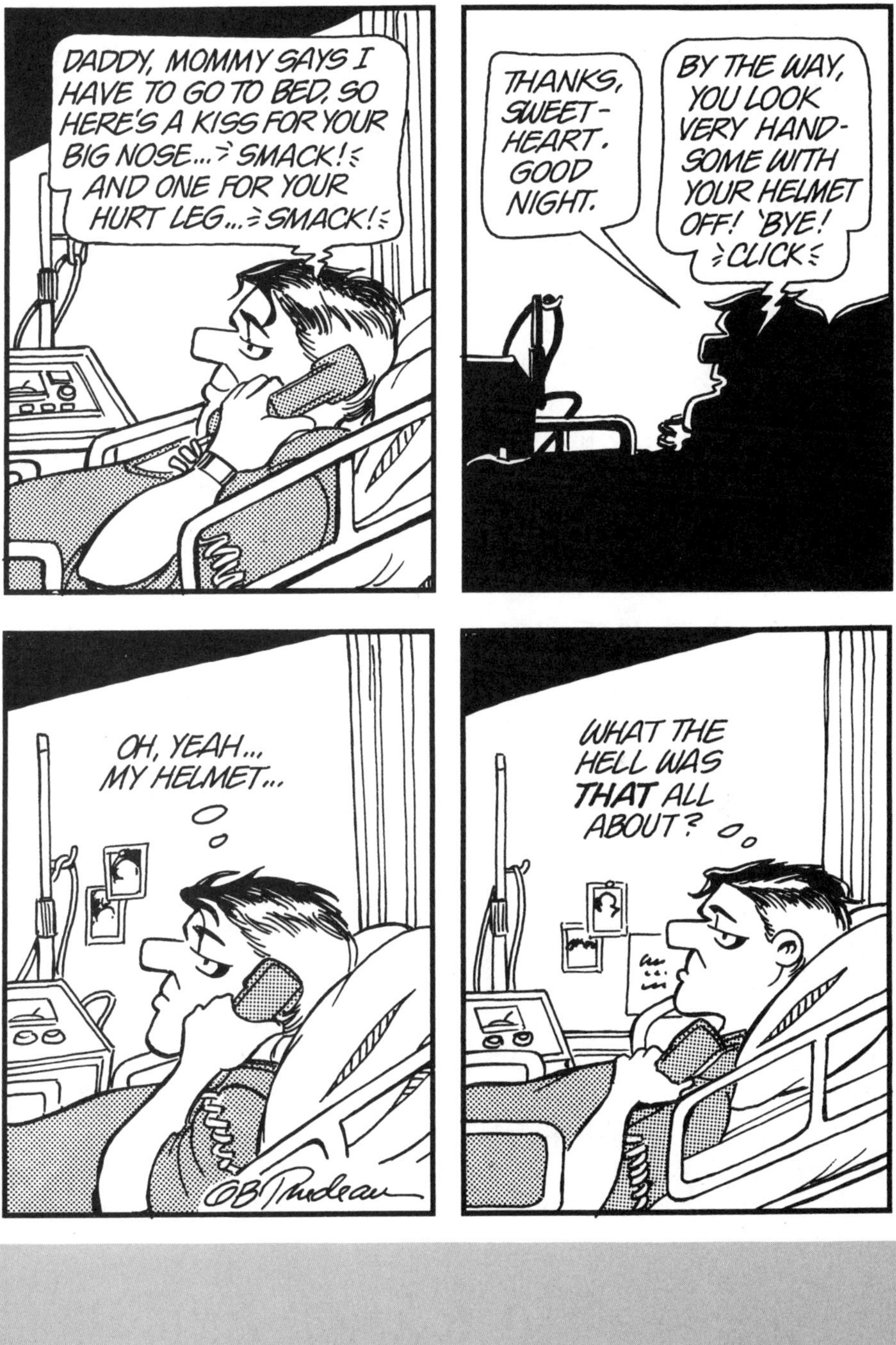
DADDY, MOMMY SAYS I HAVE TO GO TO BED, SO HERE'S A KISS FOR YOUR BIG NOSE... SMACK! AND ONE FOR YOUR HURT LEG... SMACK!
THANKS, SWEET-HEART. GOOD NIGHT.
BY THE WAY, YOU LOOK VERY HAND-SOME WITH YOUR HELMET OFF! 'BYE! CLICK
OH, YEAH... MY HELMET...
WHAT THE HELL WAS THAT ALL ABOUT?
GB Trudeau

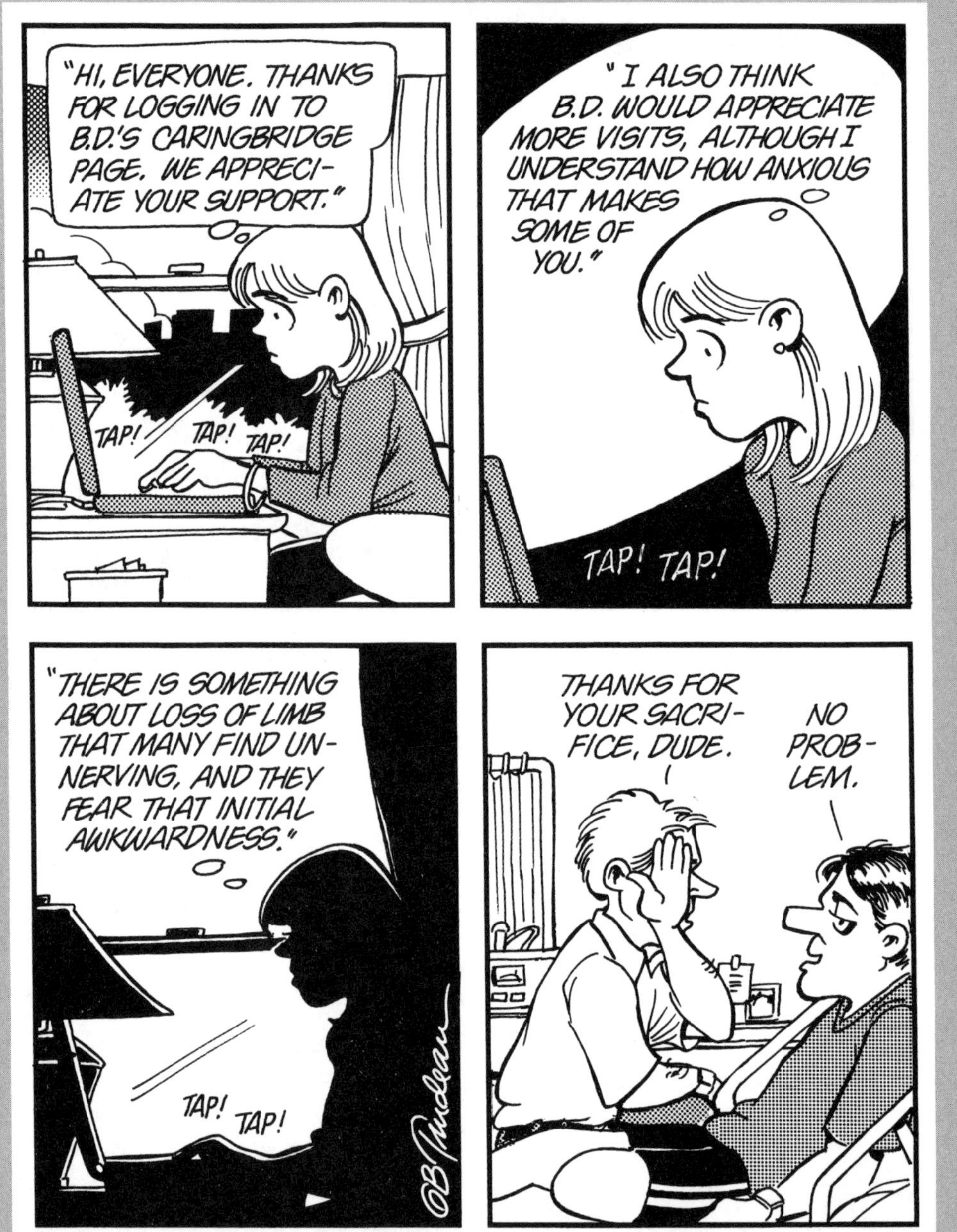
"HI, EVERYONE. THANKS FOR LOGGING IN TO B.D.'S CARINGBRIDGE PAGE. WE APPRECIATE YOUR SUPPORT."
TAP! TAP! TAP!
"I ALSO THINK B.D. WOULD APPRECIATE MORE VISITS, ALTHOUGH I UNDERSTAND HOW ANXIOUS THAT MAKES SOME OF YOU."
TAP! TAP!
"THERE IS SOMETHING ABOUT LOSS OF LIMB THAT MANY FIND UNNERVING, AND THEY FEAR THAT INITIAL AWKWARDNESS."
TAP! TAP!
THANKS FOR YOUR SACRIFICE, DUDE.
NO PROBLEM.

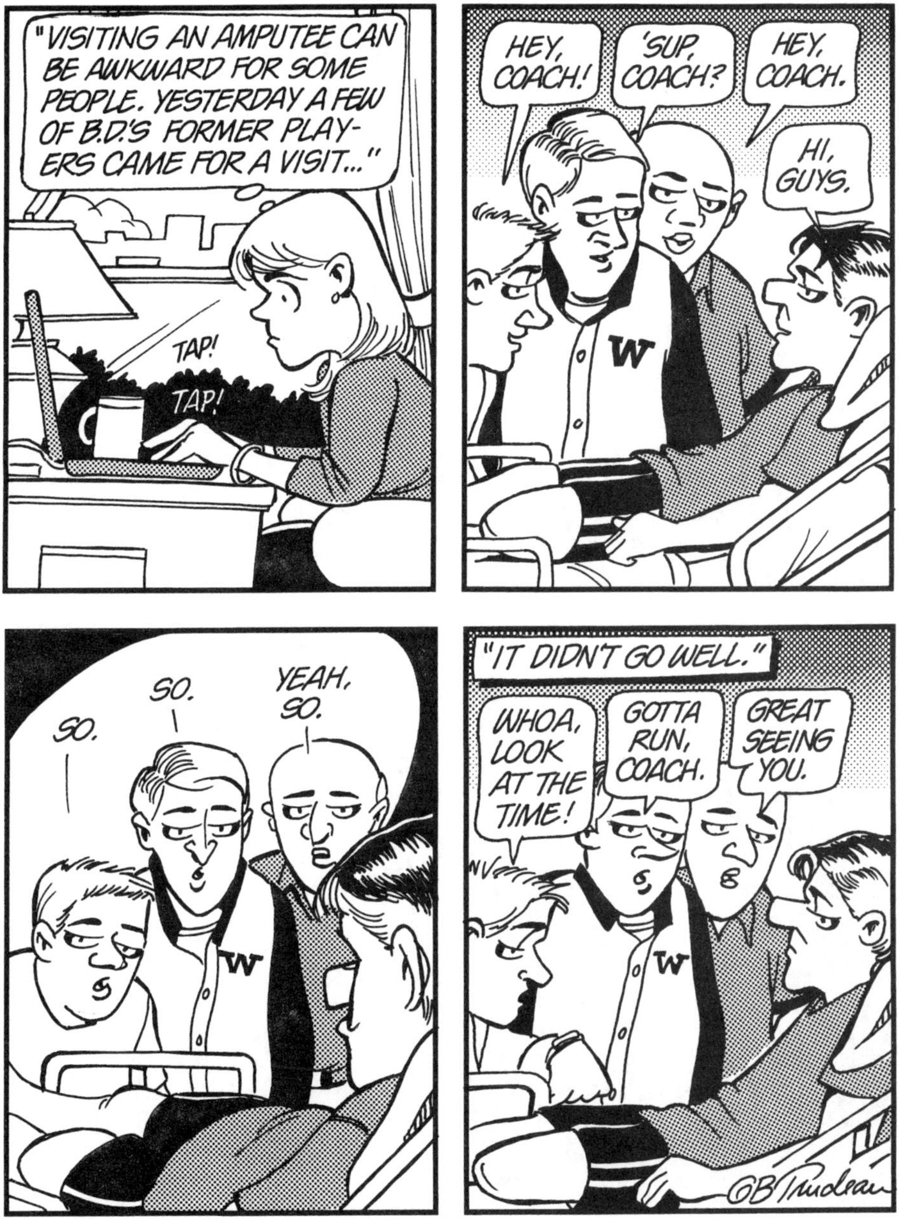
"VISITING AN AMPUTEE CAN BE AWKWARD FOR SOME PEOPLE. YESTERDAY A FEW OF B.D.'S FORMER PLAYERS CAME FOR A VISIT..."
TAP!
TAP!
HEY, COACH!
'SUP, COACH?
HEY, COACH.
HI, GUYS.
SO.
SO.
YEAH, SO.
"IT DIDN'T GO WELL."
WHOA, LOOK AT THE TIME!
GOTTA RUN, COACH.
GREAT SEEING YOU.
©B Trudeau

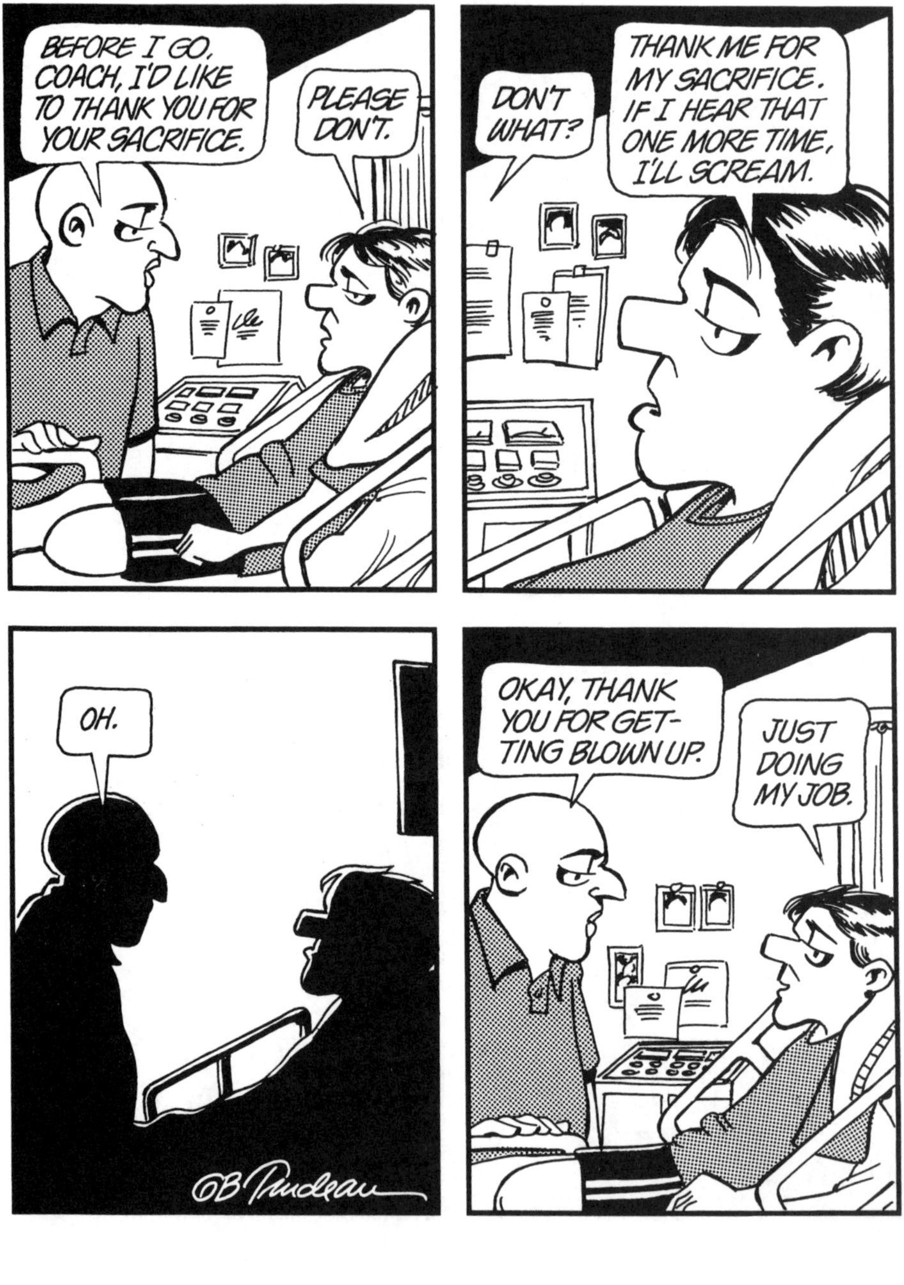
BEFORE I GO, COACH, I'D LIKE TO THANK YOU FOR YOUR SACRIFICE.
PLEASE DON'T.
DON'T WHAT?
THANK ME FOR MY SACRIFICE. IF I HEAR THAT ONE MORE TIME, I'LL SCREAM.
OH.
OKAY, THANK YOU FOR GETTING BLOWN UP.
JUST DOING MY JOB.
©B Trudeau

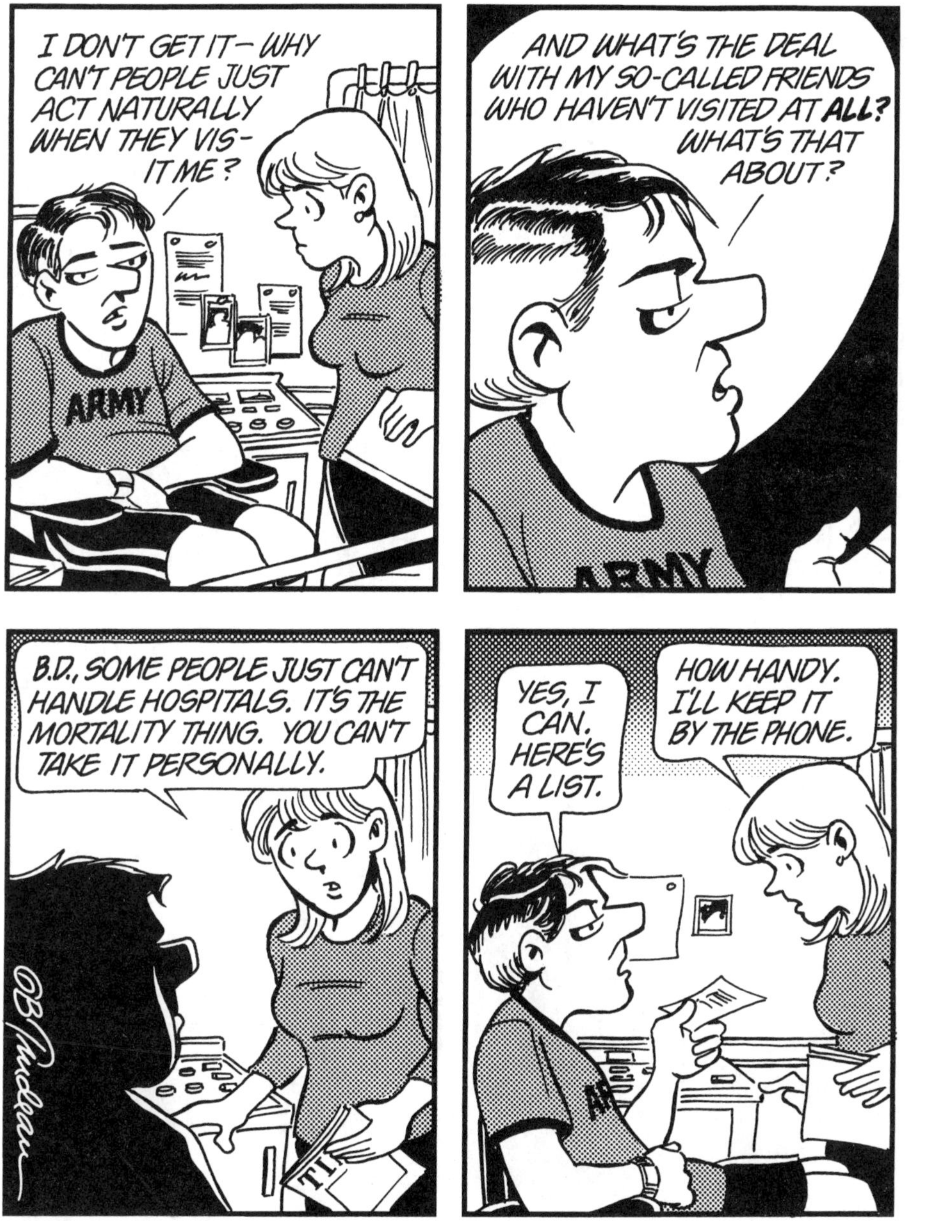
I DON'T GET IT— WHY CAN'T PEOPLE JUST ACT NATURALLY WHEN THEY VISIT ME?
ARMY
AND WHAT'S THE DEAL WITH MY SO-CALLED FRIENDS WHO HAVEN'T VISITED AT **ALL?** WHAT'S THAT ABOUT?
ARMY
B.D., SOME PEOPLE JUST CAN'T HANDLE HOSPITALS. IT'S THE MORTALITY THING. YOU CAN'T TAKE IT PERSONALLY.
©B Trudeau
YES, I CAN. HERE'S A LIST.
HOW HANDY. I'LL KEEP IT BY THE PHONE.

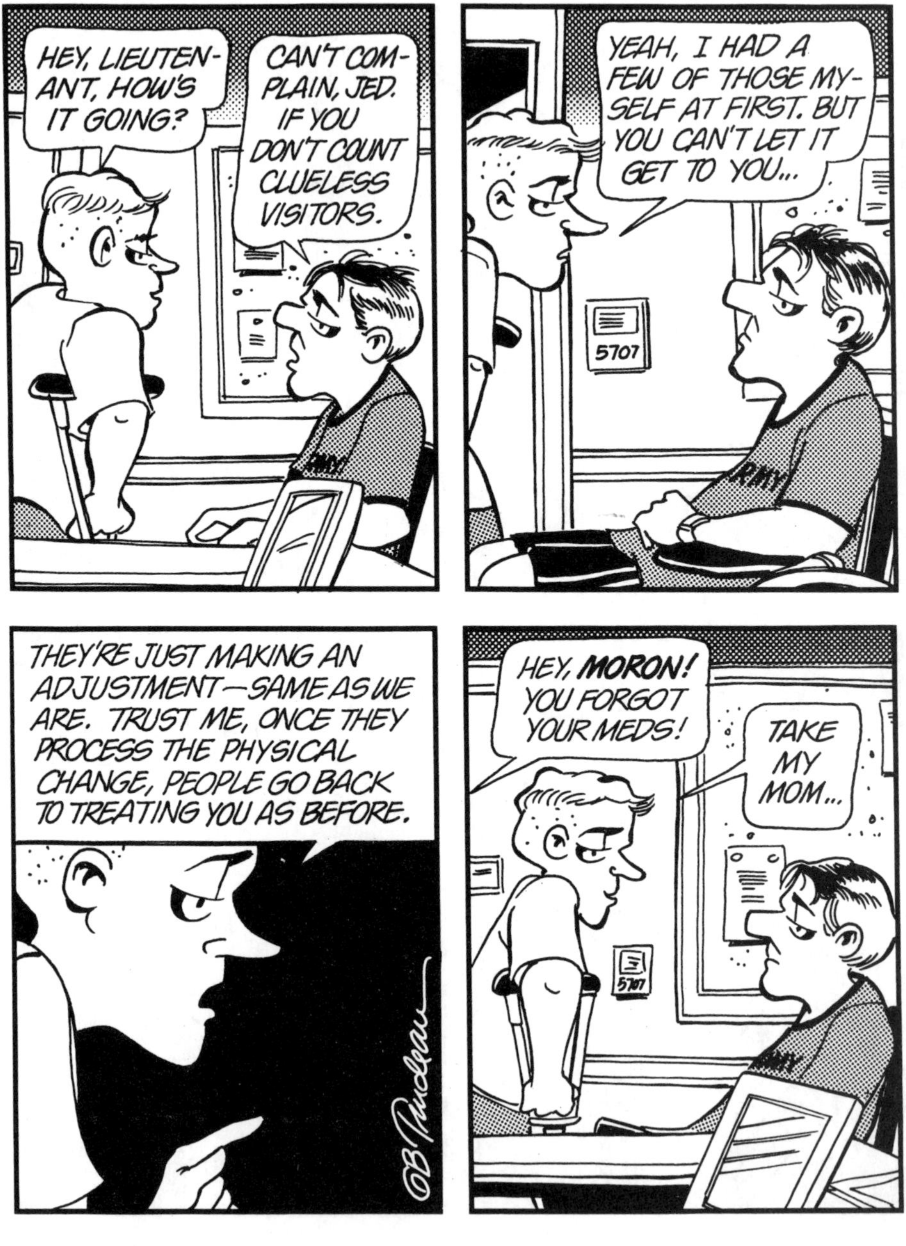

HEY, LIEUTEN-ANT, HOW'S IT GOING?
CAN'T COM-PLAIN, JED. IF YOU DON'T COUNT CLUELESS VISITORS.
5707
YEAH, I HAD A FEW OF THOSE MY-SELF AT FIRST. BUT YOU CAN'T LET IT GET TO YOU...
THEY'RE JUST MAKING AN ADJUSTMENT—SAME AS WE ARE. TRUST ME, ONCE THEY PROCESS THE PHYSICAL CHANGE, PEOPLE GO BACK TO TREATING YOU AS BEFORE.
HEY, **MORON**! YOU FORGOT YOUR MEDS!
TAKE MY MOM...
5707

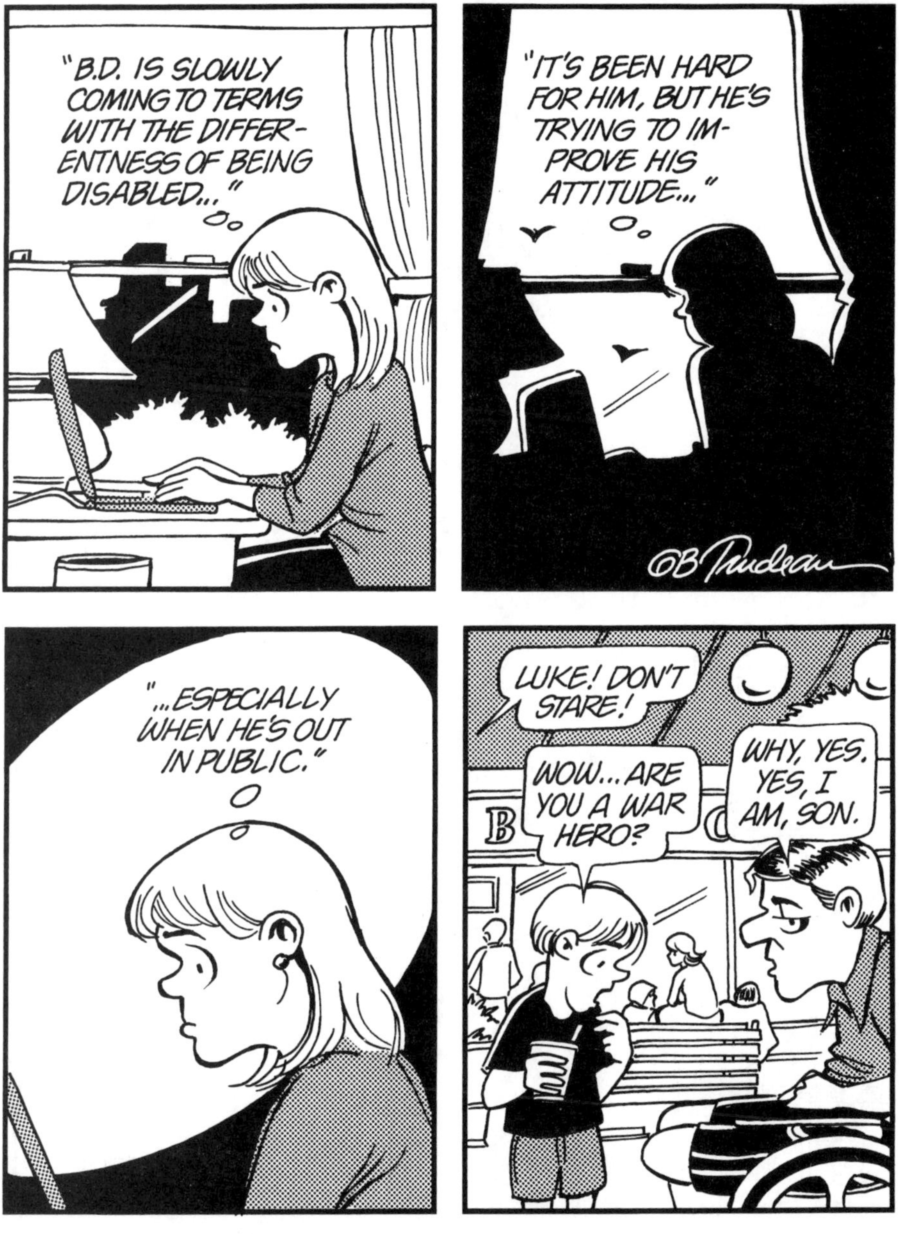
"B.D. IS SLOWLY COMING TO TERMS WITH THE DIFFER-ENTNESS OF BEING DISABLED..."
"IT'S BEEN HARD FOR HIM, BUT HE'S TRYING TO IM-PROVE HIS ATTITUDE..."
©B Trudeau
"...ESPECIALLY WHEN HE'S OUT IN PUBLIC."
LUKE! DON'T STARE!
WOW... ARE YOU A WAR HERO?
WHY, YES. YES, I AM, SON.

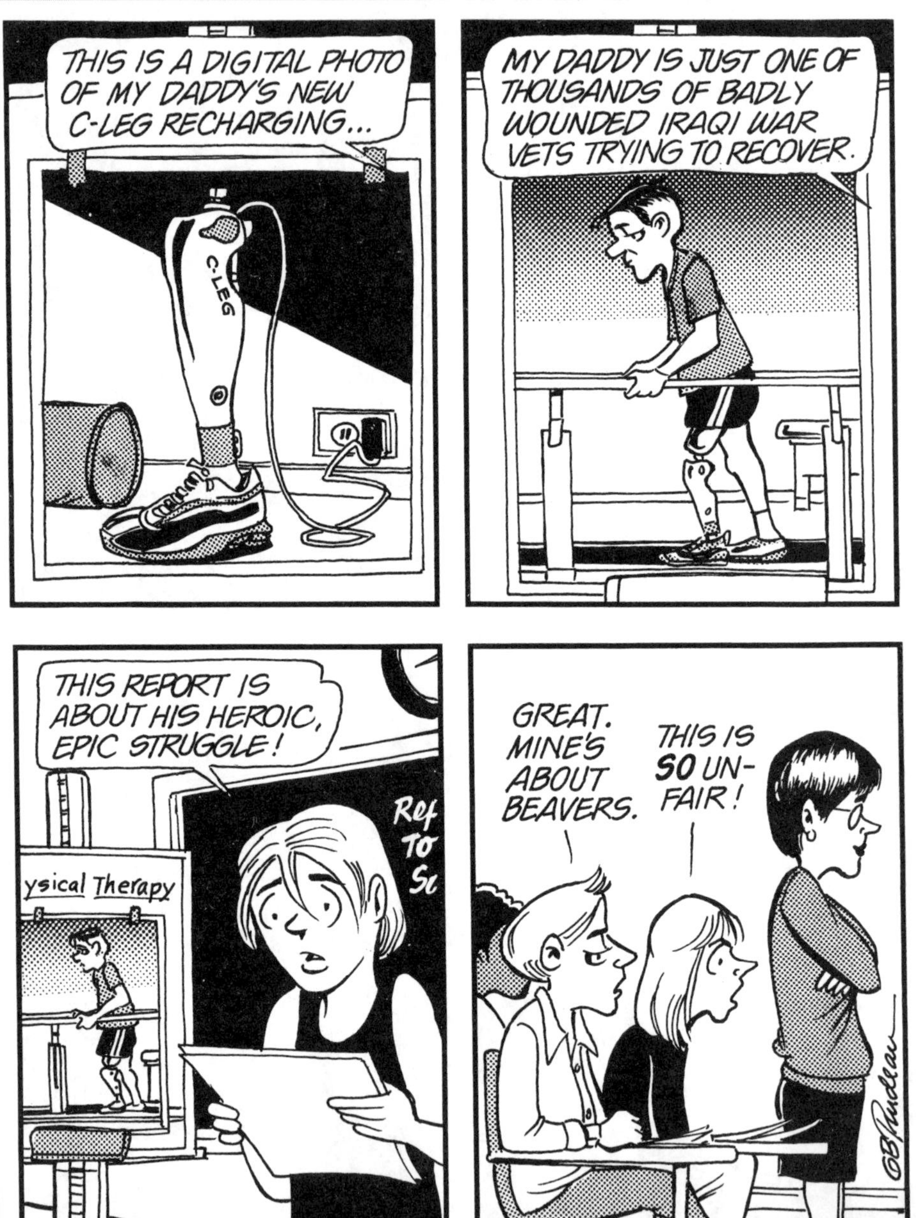
THIS IS A DIGITAL PHOTO OF MY DADDY'S NEW C-LEG RECHARGING...
C-LEG
MY DADDY IS JUST ONE OF THOUSANDS OF BADLY WOUNDED IRAQI WAR VETS TRYING TO RECOVER.
THIS REPORT IS ABOUT HIS HEROIC, EPIC STRUGGLE!
ysical Therapy
GREAT. MINE'S ABOUT BEAVERS.
THIS IS **SO** UNFAIR!
©GBTrudeau

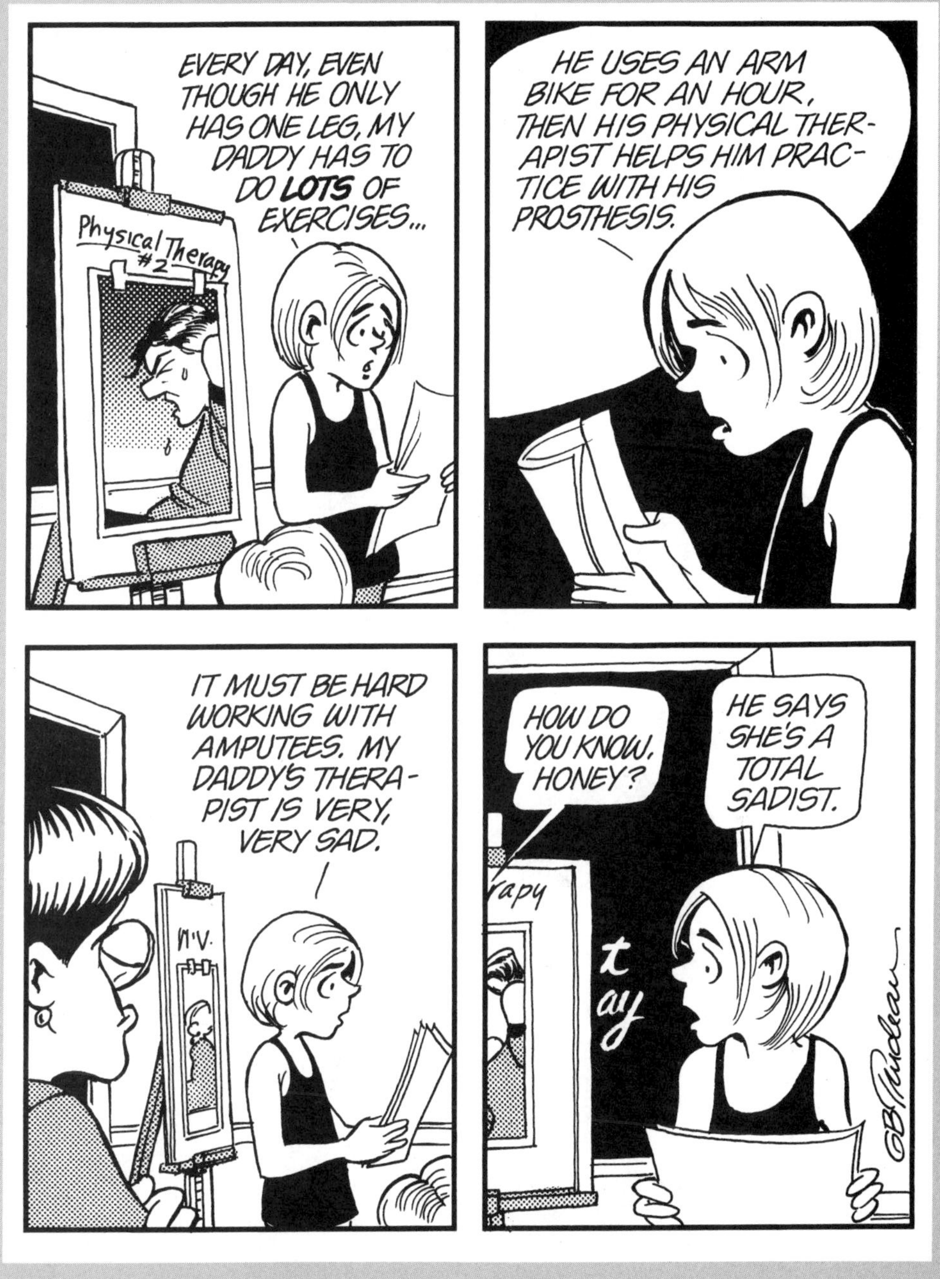
Physical Therapy #2
EVERY DAY, EVEN THOUGH HE ONLY HAS ONE LEG, MY DADDY HAS TO DO **LOTS** OF EXERCISES...
HE USES AN ARM BIKE FOR AN HOUR, THEN HIS PHYSICAL THER-APIST HELPS HIM PRAC-TICE WITH HIS PROSTHESIS.
IT MUST BE HARD WORKING WITH AMPUTEES. MY DADDY'S THERA-PIST IS VERY, VERY SAD.
HOW DO YOU KNOW, HONEY?
HE SAYS SHE'S A TOTAL SADIST.

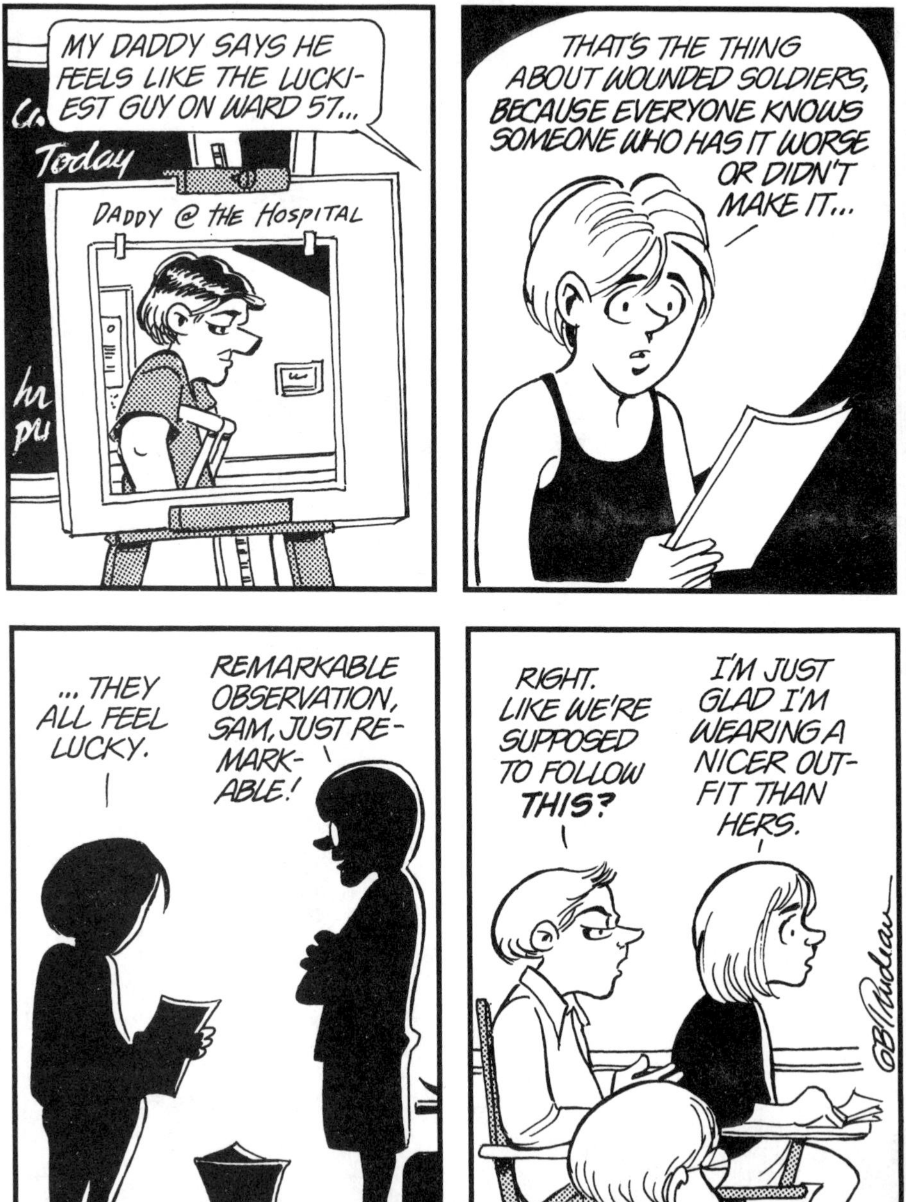
MY DADDY SAYS HE FEELS LIKE THE LUCKI-EST GUY ON WARD 57...
Today
DADDY @ THE HOSPITAL
THAT'S THE THING ABOUT WOUNDED SOLDIERS, BECAUSE EVERYONE KNOWS SOMEONE WHO HAS IT WORSE OR DIDN'T MAKE IT...
...THEY ALL FEEL LUCKY.
REMARKABLE OBSERVATION, SAM, JUST RE-MARK-ABLE!
RIGHT. LIKE WE'RE SUPPOSED TO FOLLOW THIS?
I'M JUST GLAD I'M WEARING A NICER OUT-FIT THAN HERS.
GBTrudeau

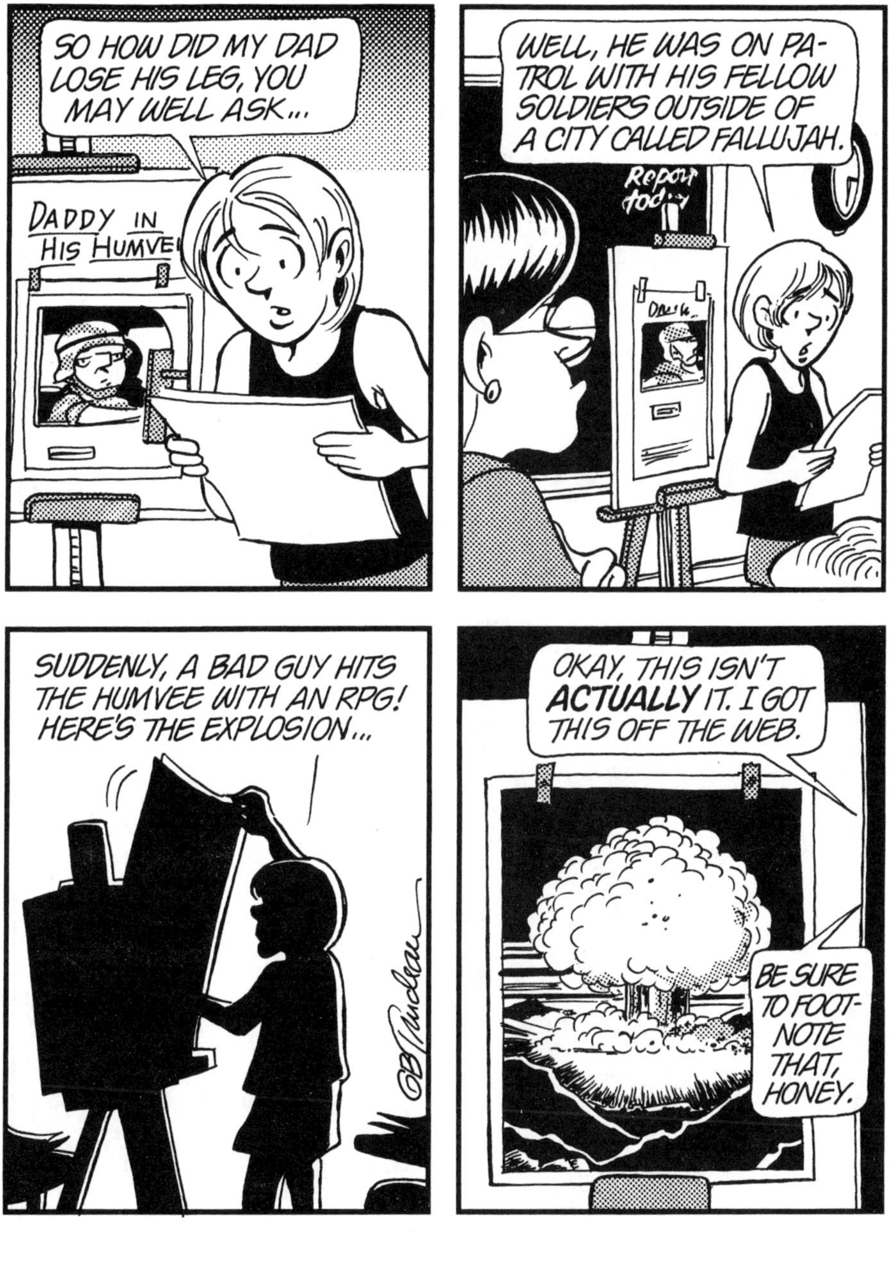
SO HOW DID MY DAD LOSE HIS LEG, YOU MAY WELL ASK...
DADDY IN HIS HUMVEE
WELL, HE WAS ON PATROL WITH HIS FELLOW SOLDIERS OUTSIDE OF A CITY CALLED FALLUJAH.
SUDDENLY, A BAD GUY HITS THE HUMVEE WITH AN RPG! HERE'S THE EXPLOSION...
OKAY, THIS ISN'T **ACTUALLY** IT. I GOT THIS OFF THE WEB.
BE SURE TO FOOTNOTE THAT, HONEY.

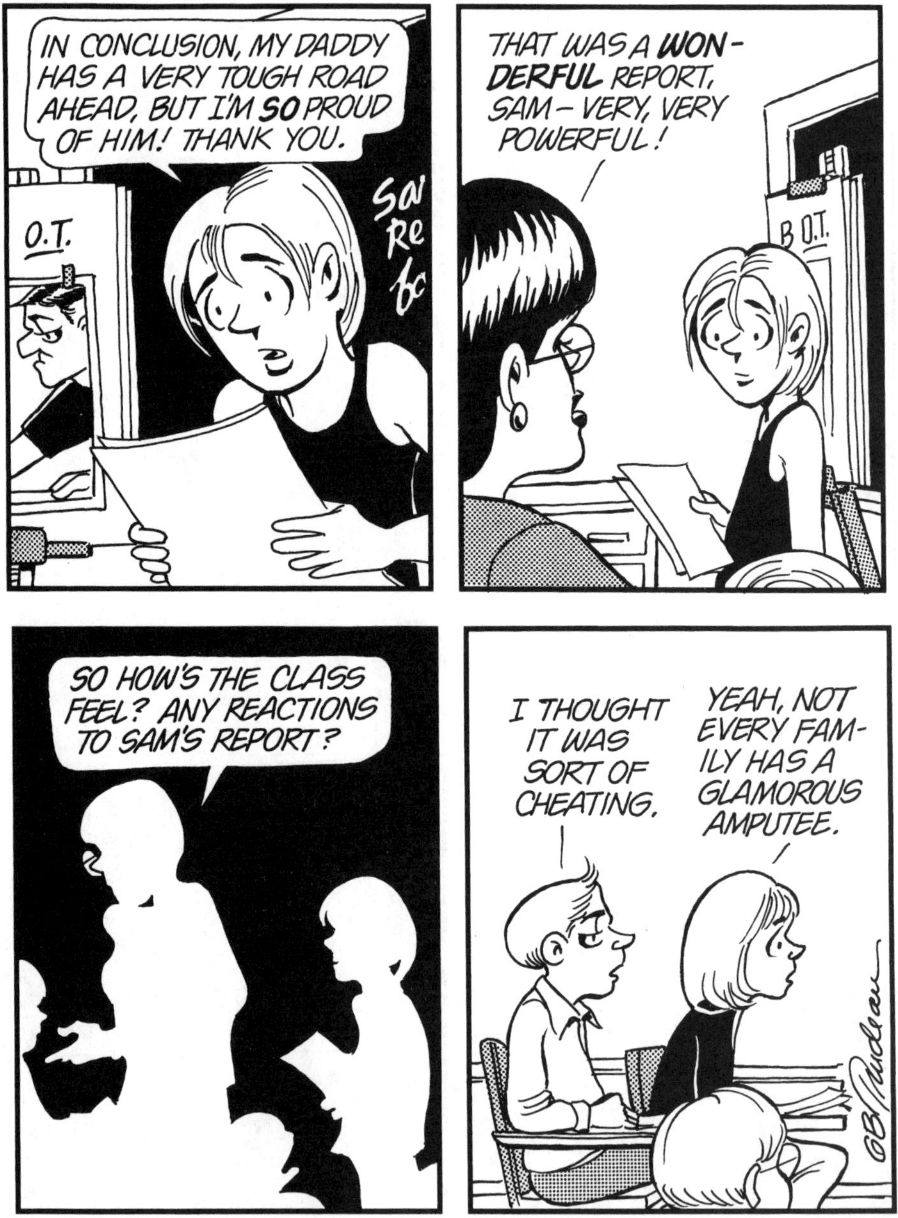
IN CONCLUSION, MY DADDY HAS A VERY TOUGH ROAD AHEAD, BUT I'M **SO** PROUD OF HIM! THANK YOU.
O.T.
THAT WAS A **WONDERFUL** REPORT, SAM – VERY, VERY POWERFUL!
B O.T.
SO HOW'S THE CLASS FEEL? ANY REACTIONS TO SAM'S REPORT?
I THOUGHT IT WAS SORT OF CHEATING.
YEAH, NOT EVERY FAMILY HAS A GLAMOROUS AMPUTEE.

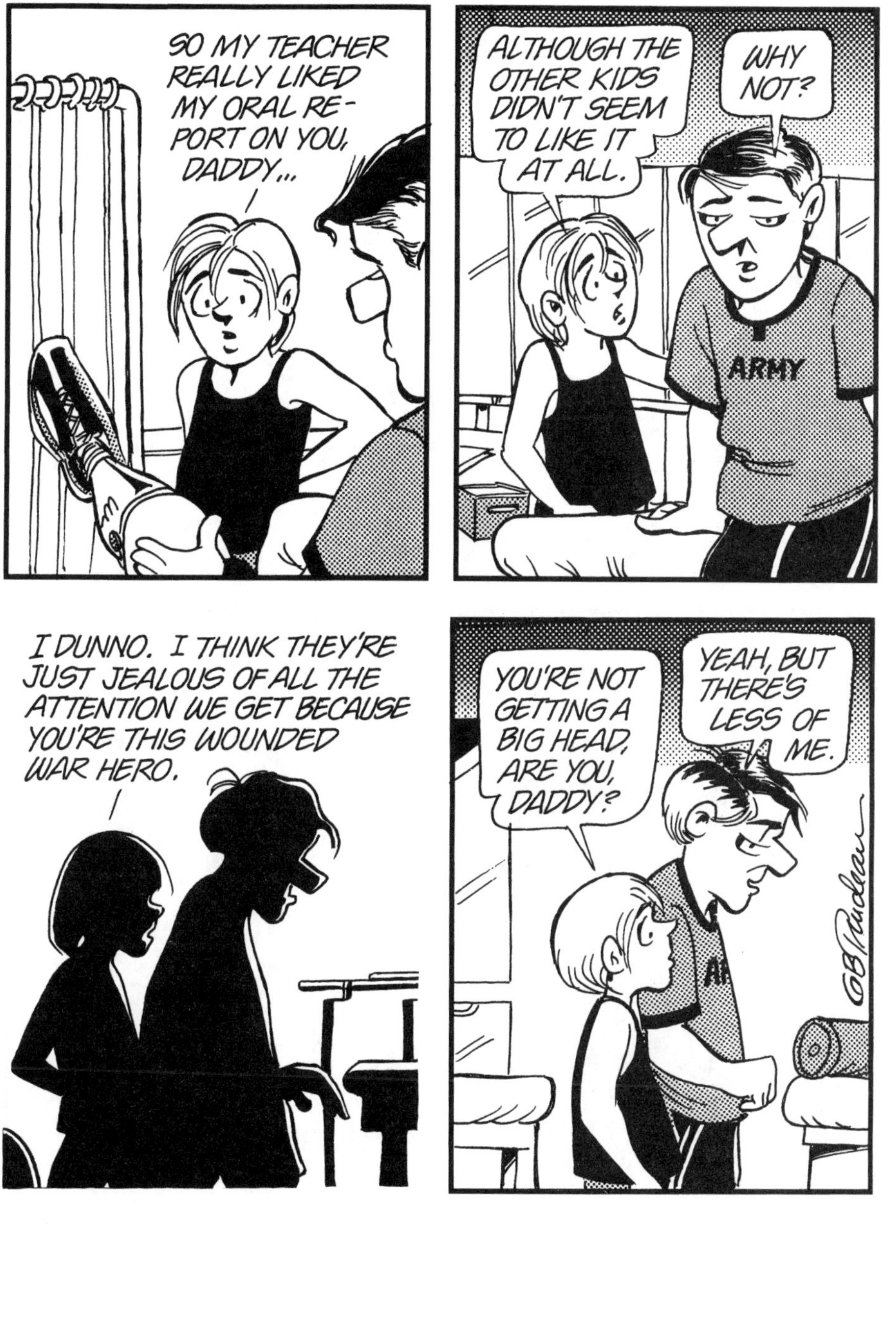
SO MY TEACHER REALLY LIKED MY ORAL RE-PORT ON YOU, DADDY...
ALTHOUGH THE OTHER KIDS DIDN'T SEEM TO LIKE IT AT ALL.
WHY NOT?
ARMY
I DUNNO. I THINK THEY'RE JUST JEALOUS OF ALL THE ATTENTION WE GET BECAUSE YOU'RE THIS WOUNDED WAR HERO.
YOU'RE NOT GETTING A BIG HEAD, ARE YOU, DADDY?
YEAH, BUT THERE'S LESS OF ME.
GBTrudeau

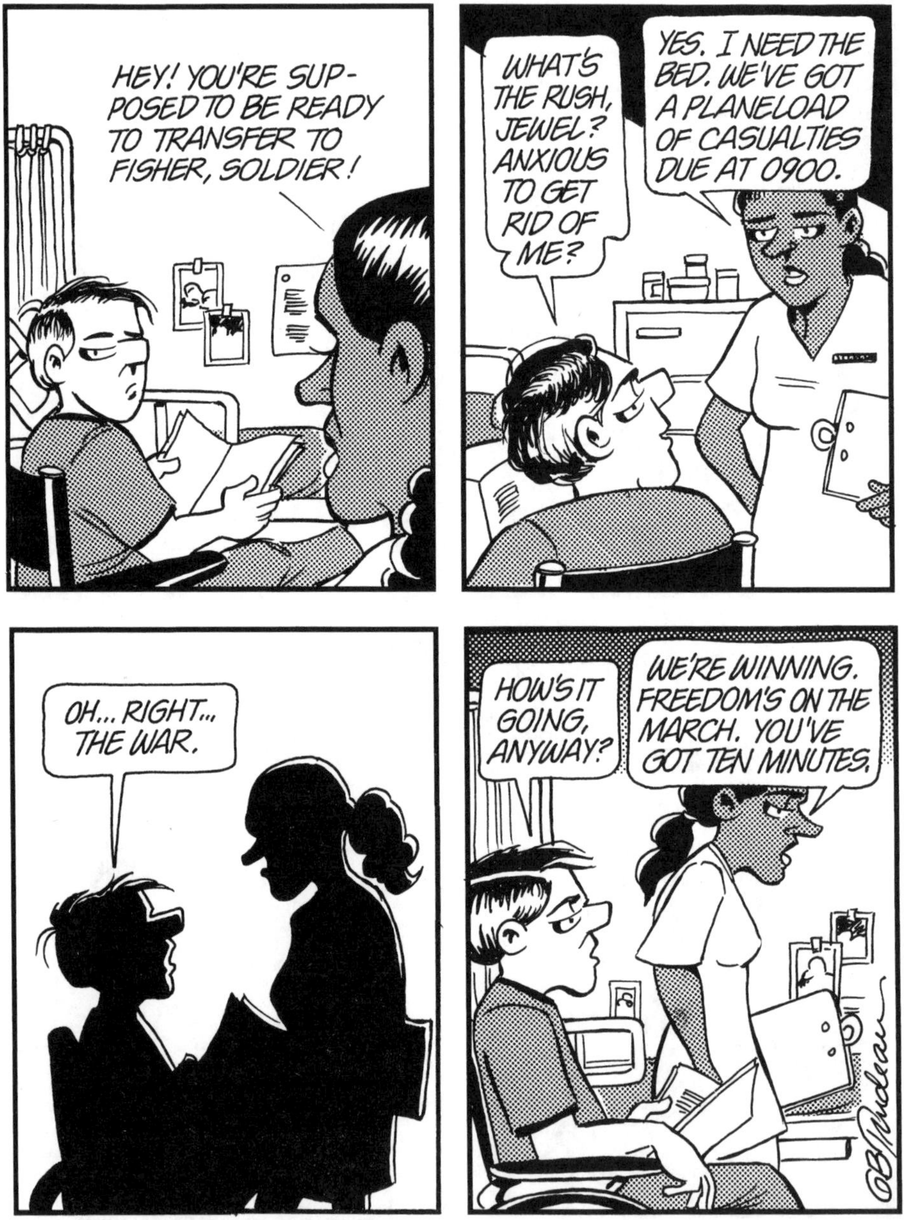
HEY! YOU'RE SUP-POSED TO BE READY TO TRANSFER TO FISHER, SOLDIER!
WHAT'S THE RUSH, JEWEL? ANXIOUS TO GET RID OF ME?
YES. I NEED THE BED. WE'VE GOT A PLANELOAD OF CASUALTIES DUE AT 0900.
OH... RIGHT... THE WAR.
HOW'S IT GOING, ANYWAY?
WE'RE WINNING. FREEDOM'S ON THE MARCH. YOU'VE GOT TEN MINUTES.
GB Trudeau

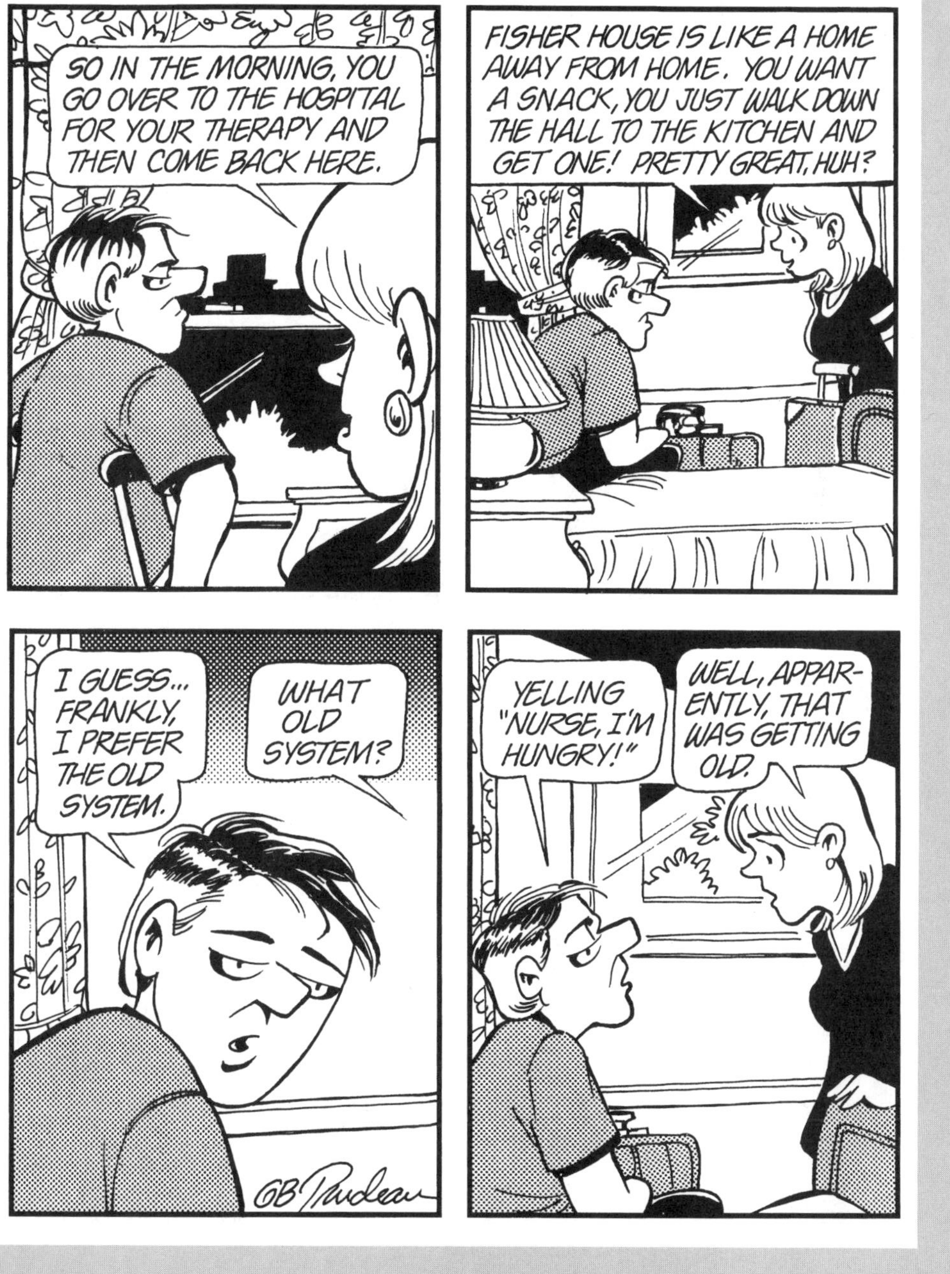
SO IN THE MORNING, YOU GO OVER TO THE HOSPITAL FOR YOUR THERAPY AND THEN COME BACK HERE.
FISHER HOUSE IS LIKE A HOME AWAY FROM HOME. YOU WANT A SNACK, YOU JUST WALK DOWN THE HALL TO THE KITCHEN AND GET ONE! PRETTY GREAT, HUH?
I GUESS... FRANKLY, I PREFER THE OLD SYSTEM.
WHAT OLD SYSTEM?
GB Trudeau
YELLING "NURSE, I'M HUNGRY!"
WELL, APPARENTLY, THAT WAS GETTING OLD.

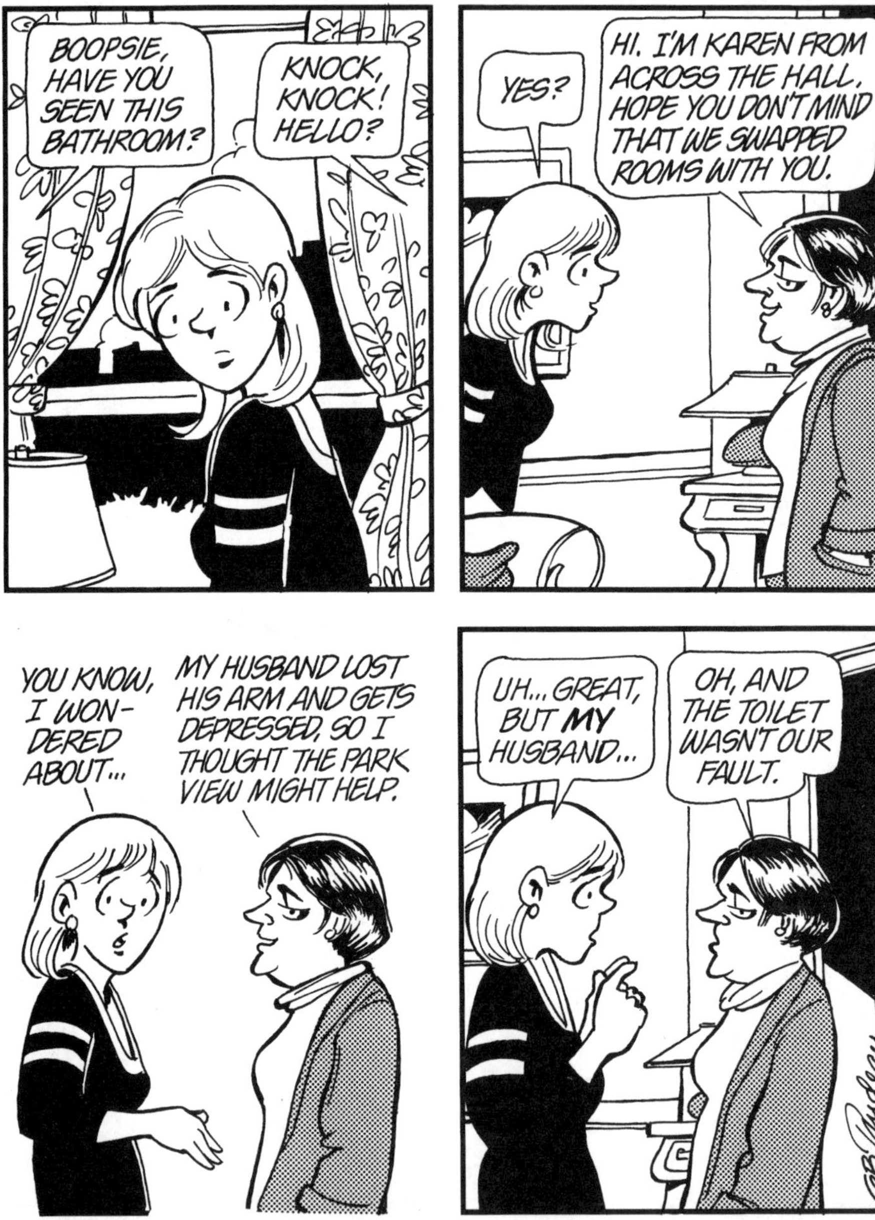
BOOPSIE, HAVE YOU SEEN THIS BATHROOM?
KNOCK, KNOCK! HELLO?
YES?
HI. I'M KAREN FROM ACROSS THE HALL. HOPE YOU DON'T MIND THAT WE SWAPPED ROOMS WITH YOU.
YOU KNOW, I WON-DERED ABOUT...
MY HUSBAND LOST HIS ARM AND GETS DEPRESSED, SO I THOUGHT THE PARK VIEW MIGHT HELP.
UH... GREAT, BUT **MY** HUSBAND...
OH, AND THE TOILET WASN'T OUR FAULT.
GBTrudeau

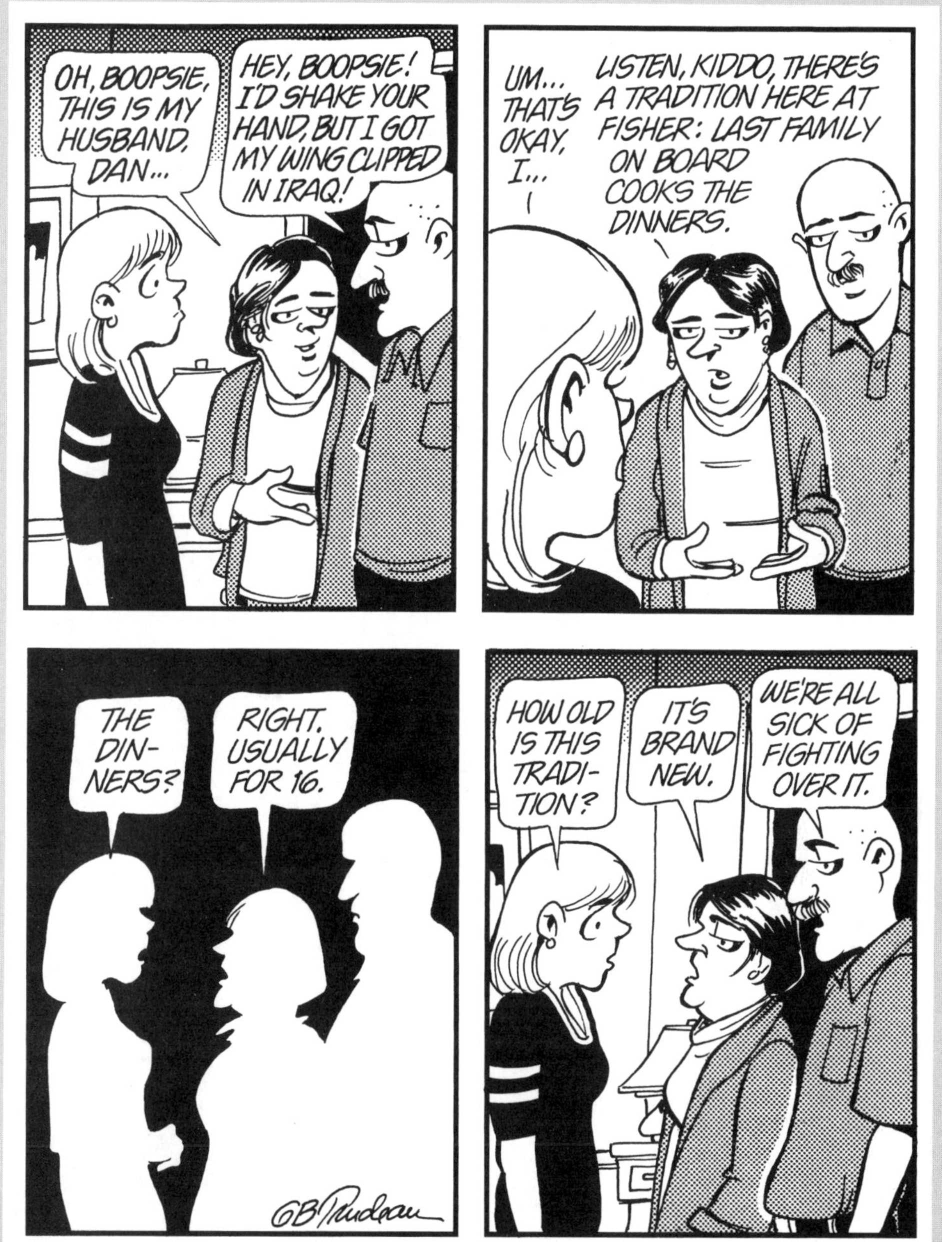
OH, BOOPSIE, THIS IS MY HUSBAND, DAN...
HEY, BOOPSIE! I'D SHAKE YOUR HAND, BUT I GOT MY WING CLIPPED IN IRAQ!
UM... THAT'S OKAY, I...
LISTEN, KIDDO, THERE'S A TRADITION HERE AT FISHER: LAST FAMILY ON BOARD COOKS THE DINNERS.
THE DIN-NERS?
RIGHT. USUALLY FOR 16.
HOW OLD IS THIS TRADI-TION?
IT'S BRAND NEW.
WE'RE ALL SICK OF FIGHTING OVER IT.
GB Trudeau

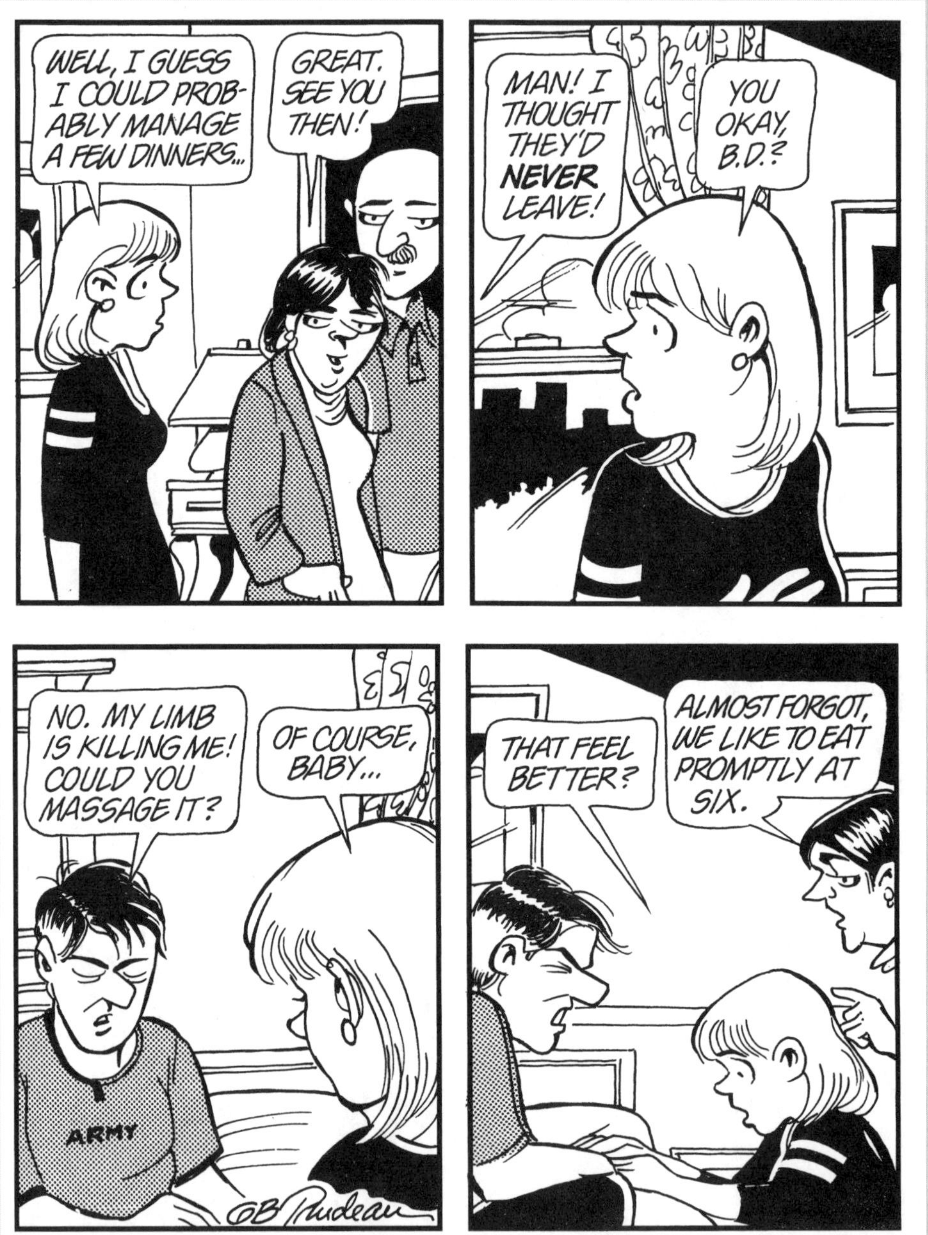
WELL, I GUESS I COULD PROB-ABLY MANAGE A FEW DINNERS...
GREAT. SEE YOU THEN!
MAN! I THOUGHT THEY'D **NEVER** LEAVE!
YOU OKAY, B.D.?
NO. MY LIMB IS KILLING ME! COULD YOU MASSAGE IT?
OF COURSE, BABY...
ARMY
GB Trudeau
THAT FEEL BETTER?
ALMOST FORGOT, WE LIKE TO EAT PROMPTLY AT SIX.

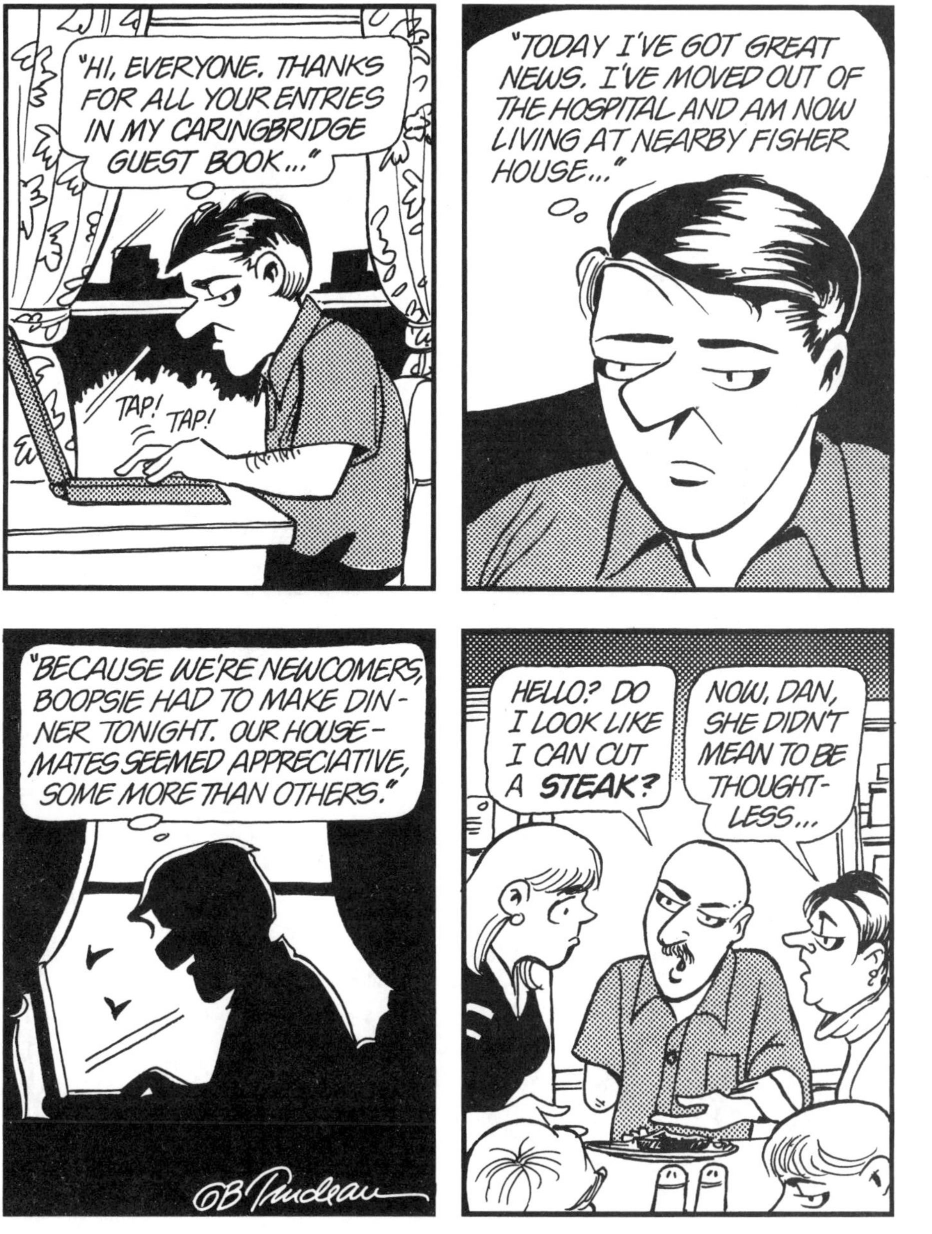

"HI, EVERYONE. THANKS FOR ALL YOUR ENTRIES IN MY CARINGBRIDGE GUEST BOOK..."
TAP! TAP!
"TODAY I'VE GOT GREAT NEWS. I'VE MOVED OUT OF THE HOSPITAL AND AM NOW LIVING AT NEARBY FISHER HOUSE..."
"BECAUSE WE'RE NEWCOMERS, BOOPSIE HAD TO MAKE DINNER TONIGHT. OUR HOUSEMATES SEEMED APPRECIATIVE, SOME MORE THAN OTHERS."
©B Trudeau
HELLO? DO I LOOK LIKE I CAN CUT A STEAK?
NOW, DAN, SHE DIDN'T MEAN TO BE THOUGHTLESS...

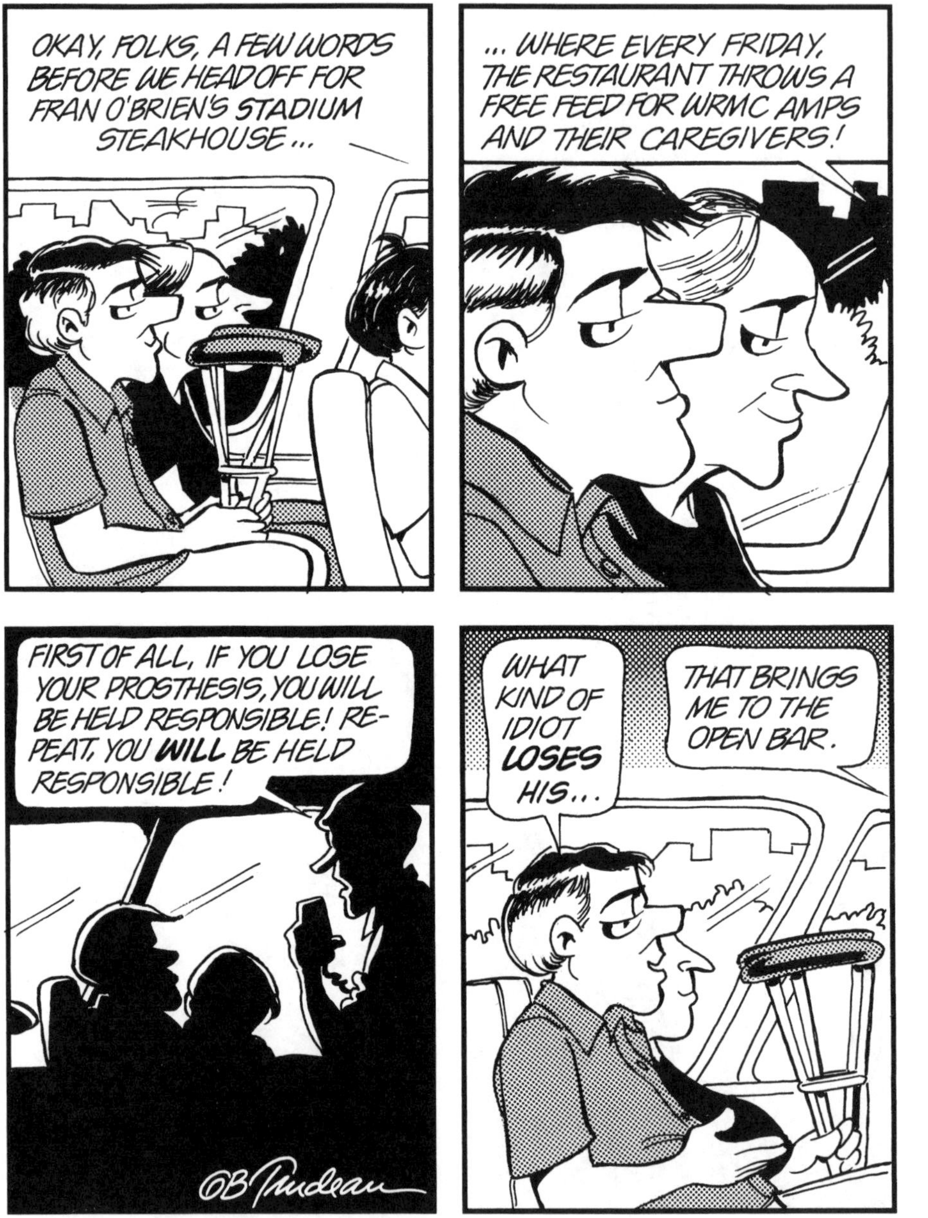
OKAY, FOLKS, A FEW WORDS BEFORE WE HEAD OFF FOR FRAN O'BRIEN'S STADIUM STEAKHOUSE...
... WHERE EVERY FRIDAY, THE RESTAURANT THROWS A FREE FEED FOR WRMC AMPS AND THEIR CAREGIVERS!
FIRST OF ALL, IF YOU LOSE YOUR PROSTHESIS, YOU WILL BE HELD RESPONSIBLE! RE-PEAT, YOU WILL BE HELD RESPONSIBLE!
©B Trudeau
WHAT KIND OF IDIOT LOSES HIS...
THAT BRINGS ME TO THE OPEN BAR.

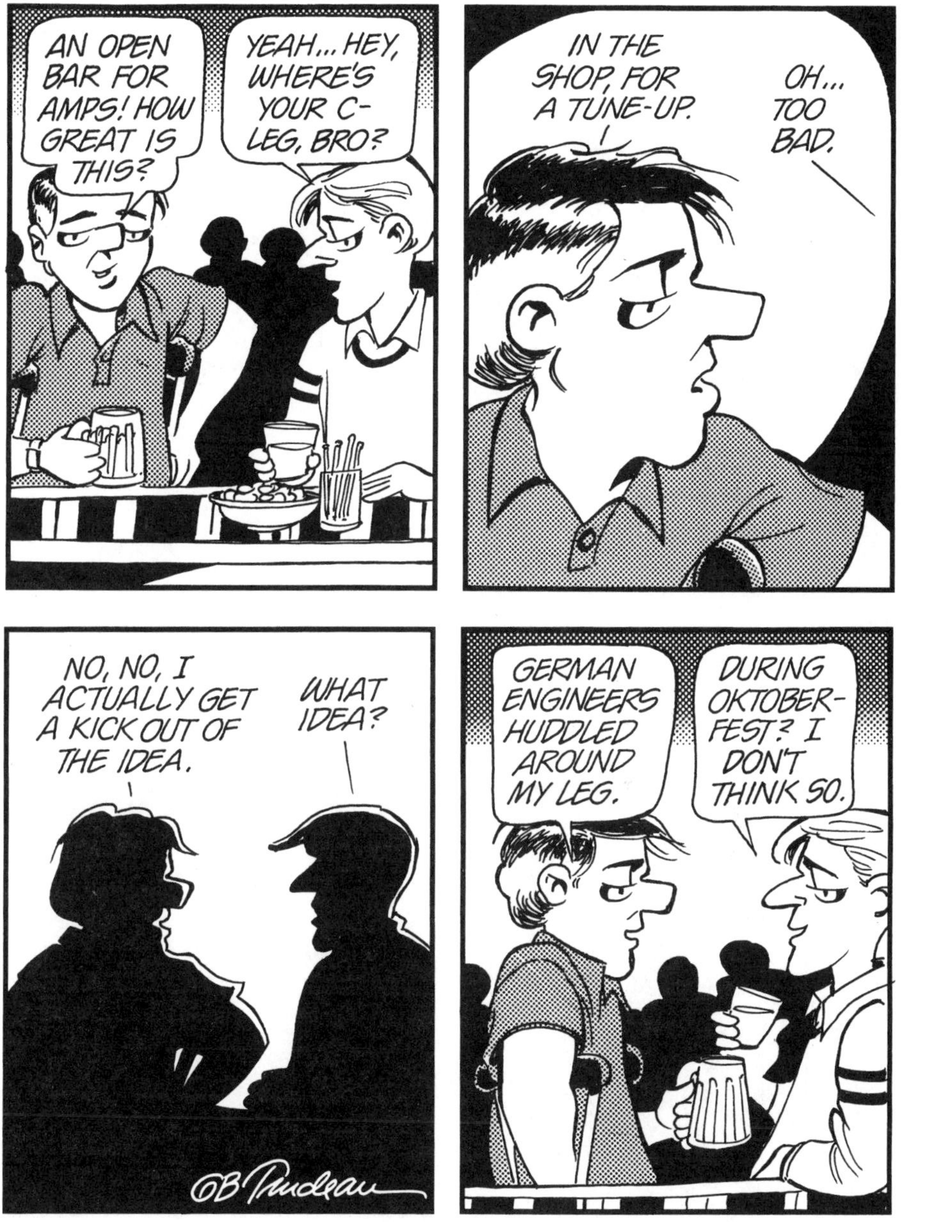
AN OPEN BAR FOR AMPS! HOW GREAT IS THIS?
YEAH... HEY, WHERE'S YOUR C-LEG, BRO?
IN THE SHOP, FOR A TUNE-UP.
OH... TOO BAD.
NO, NO, I ACTUALLY GET A KICK OUT OF THE IDEA.
WHAT IDEA?
GERMAN ENGINEERS HUDDLED AROUND MY LEG.
DURING OKTOBERFEST? I DON'T THINK SO.
©B Trudeau

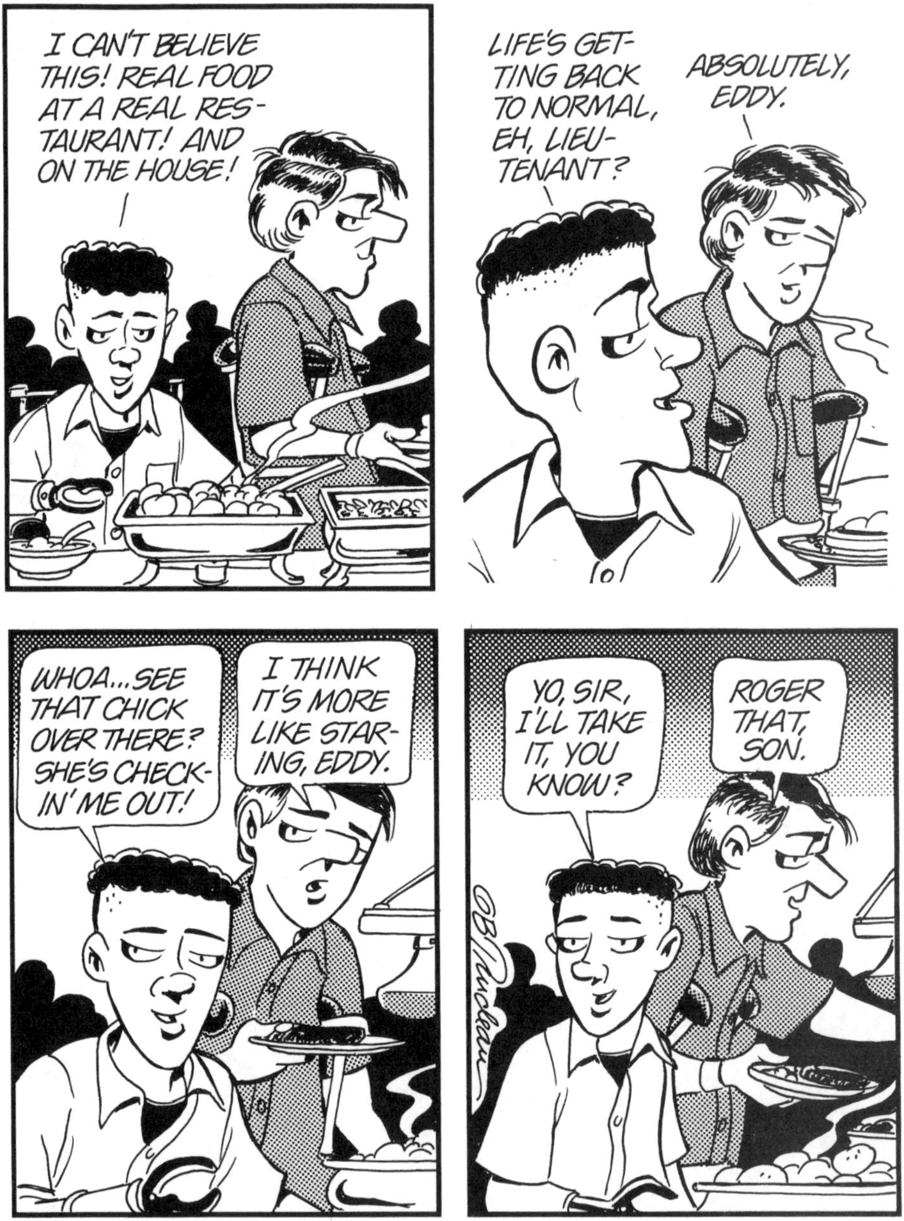
I CAN'T BELIEVE THIS! REAL FOOD AT A REAL RESTAURANT! AND ON THE HOUSE!
LIFE'S GETTING BACK TO NORMAL, EH, LIEUTENANT?
ABSOLUTELY, EDDY.
WHOA...SEE THAT CHICK OVER THERE? SHE'S CHECKIN' ME OUT!
I THINK IT'S MORE LIKE STARING, EDDY.
YO, SIR, I'LL TAKE IT, YOU KNOW?
ROGER THAT, SON.
GB Trudeau

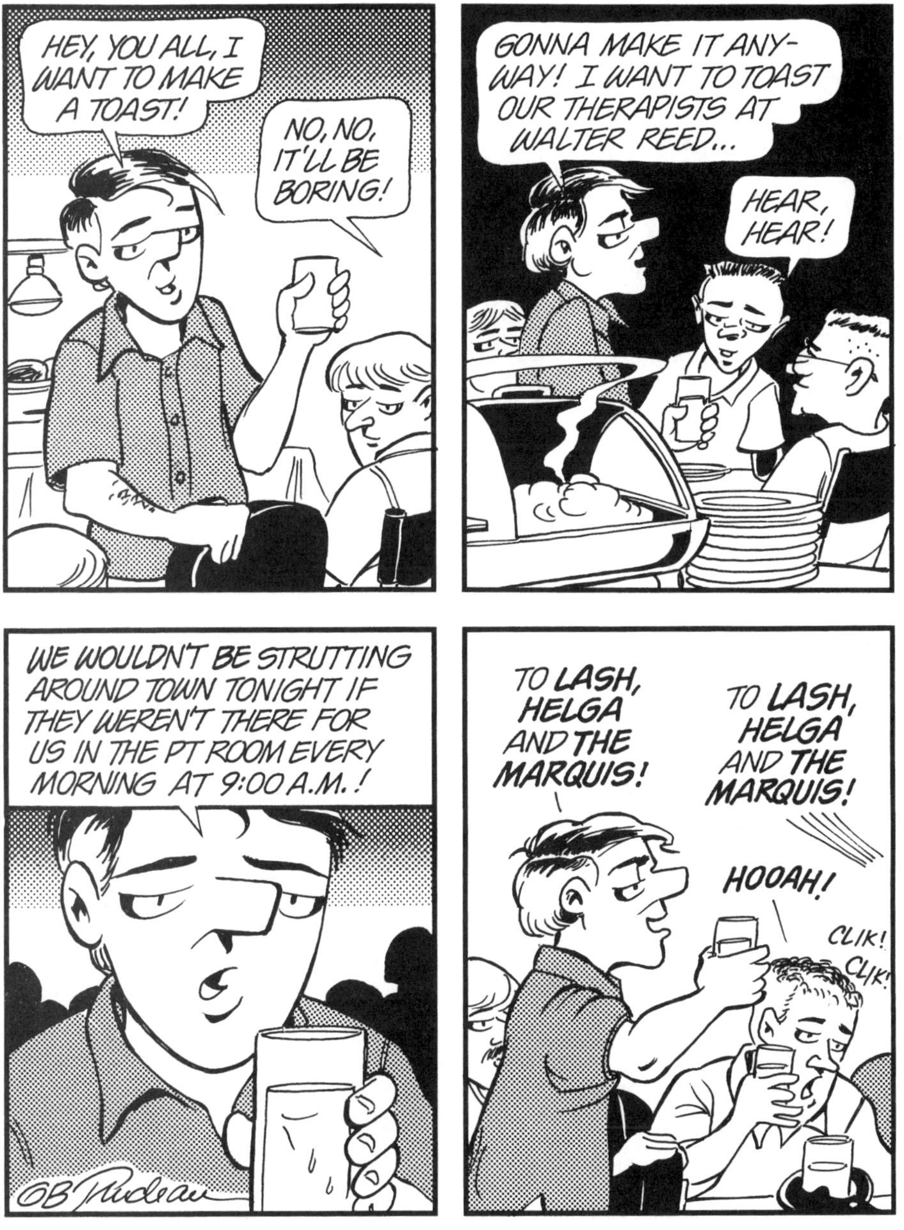
HEY, YOU ALL, I WANT TO MAKE A TOAST!
NO, NO, IT'LL BE BORING!
GONNA MAKE IT ANY-WAY! I WANT TO TOAST OUR THERAPISTS AT WALTER REED...
HEAR, HEAR!
WE WOULDN'T BE STRUTTING AROUND TOWN TONIGHT IF THEY WEREN'T THERE FOR US IN THE PT ROOM EVERY MORNING AT 9:00 A.M.!
TO LASH, HELGA AND THE MARQUIS!
TO LASH, HELGA AND THE MARQUIS!
HOOAH!
CLIK!
CLIK!
GB Trudeau

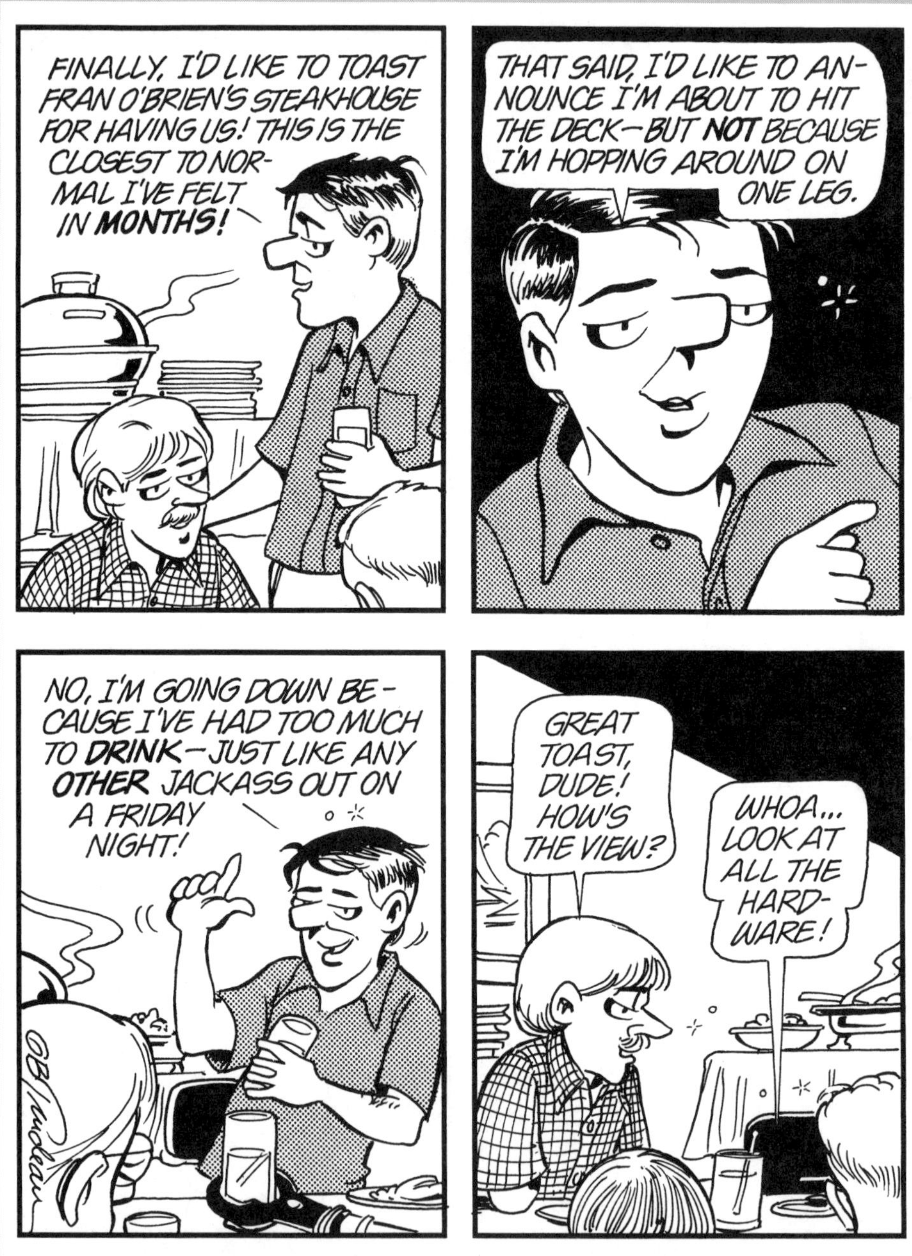
FINALLY, I'D LIKE TO TOAST FRAN O'BRIEN'S STEAKHOUSE FOR HAVING US! THIS IS THE CLOSEST TO NORMAL I'VE FELT IN MONTHS!
THAT SAID, I'D LIKE TO ANNOUNCE I'M ABOUT TO HIT THE DECK—BUT NOT BECAUSE I'M HOPPING AROUND ON ONE LEG.
NO, I'M GOING DOWN BECAUSE I'VE HAD TOO MUCH TO DRINK—JUST LIKE ANY OTHER JACKASS OUT ON A FRIDAY NIGHT!
GREAT TOAST, DUDE! HOW'S THE VIEW?
WHOA... LOOK AT ALL THE HARDWARE!

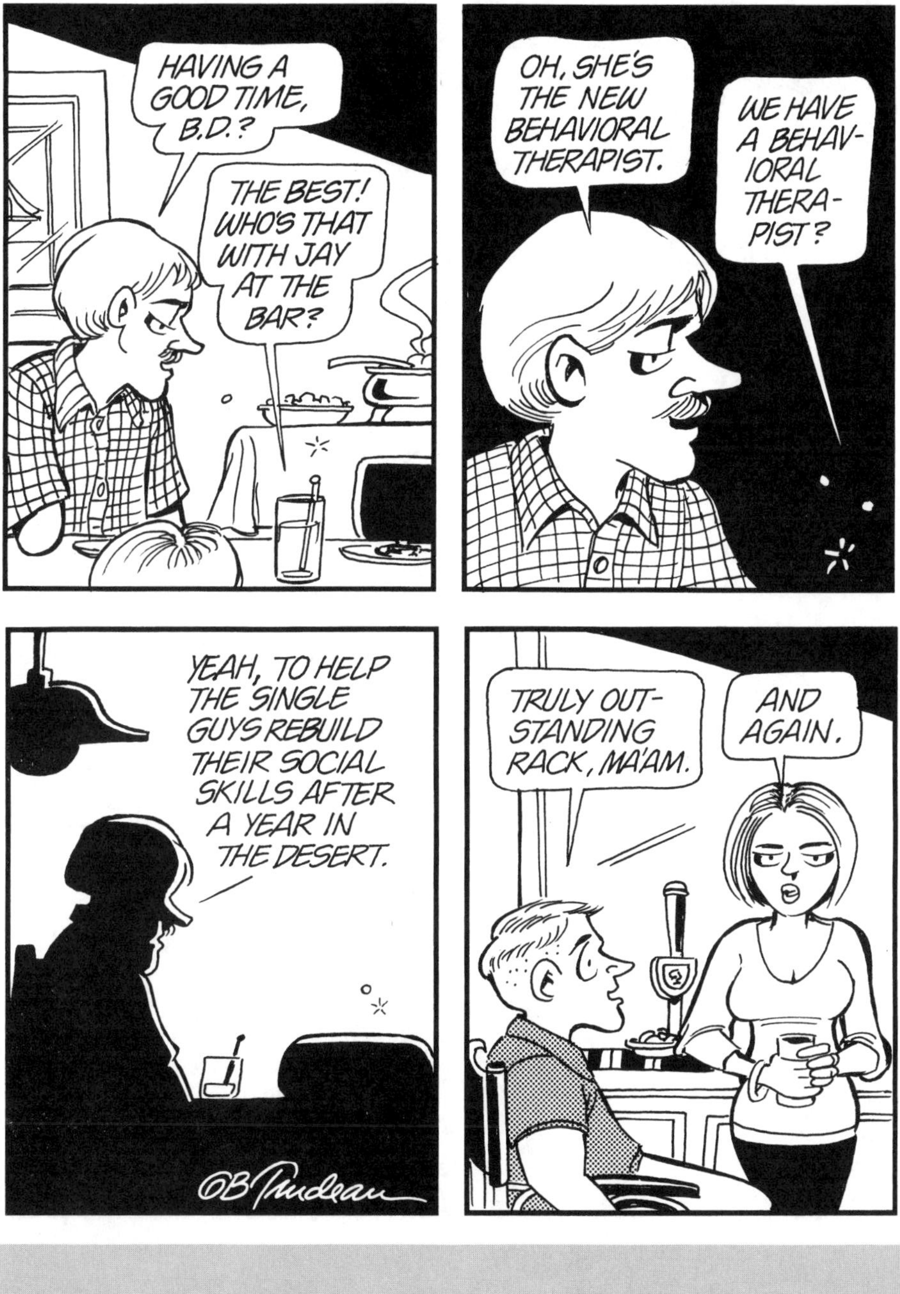
HAVING A GOOD TIME, B.D.?
THE BEST! WHO'S THAT WITH JAY AT THE BAR?
OH, SHE'S THE NEW BEHAVIORAL THERAPIST.
WE HAVE A BEHAVIORAL THERAPIST?
YEAH, TO HELP THE SINGLE GUYS REBUILD THEIR SOCIAL SKILLS AFTER A YEAR IN THE DESERT.
©B Trudeau
TRULY OUTSTANDING RACK, MA'AM.
AND AGAIN.

B.D.?
HEY, BABE! WHERE ARE YOU?
I'M AT FISHER— WHERE ARE YOU?
AT O'BRIEN'S. I GOT DRAFTED FOR BAR DUTY AT TONIGHT'S AMP PARTY.
BAR-KEEP!
HOLD ON A SEC, BOOPSIE...
ANOTHER SHOT FOR ME, AND ONE FOR MY LITTLE FRIEND!
WHICH ONE OF YOU IS DRIVING?

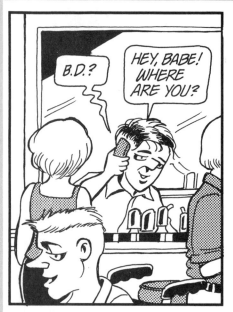

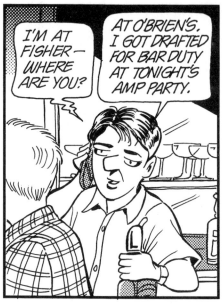

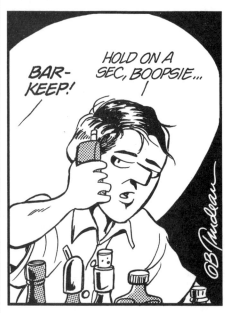

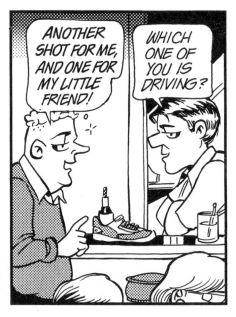

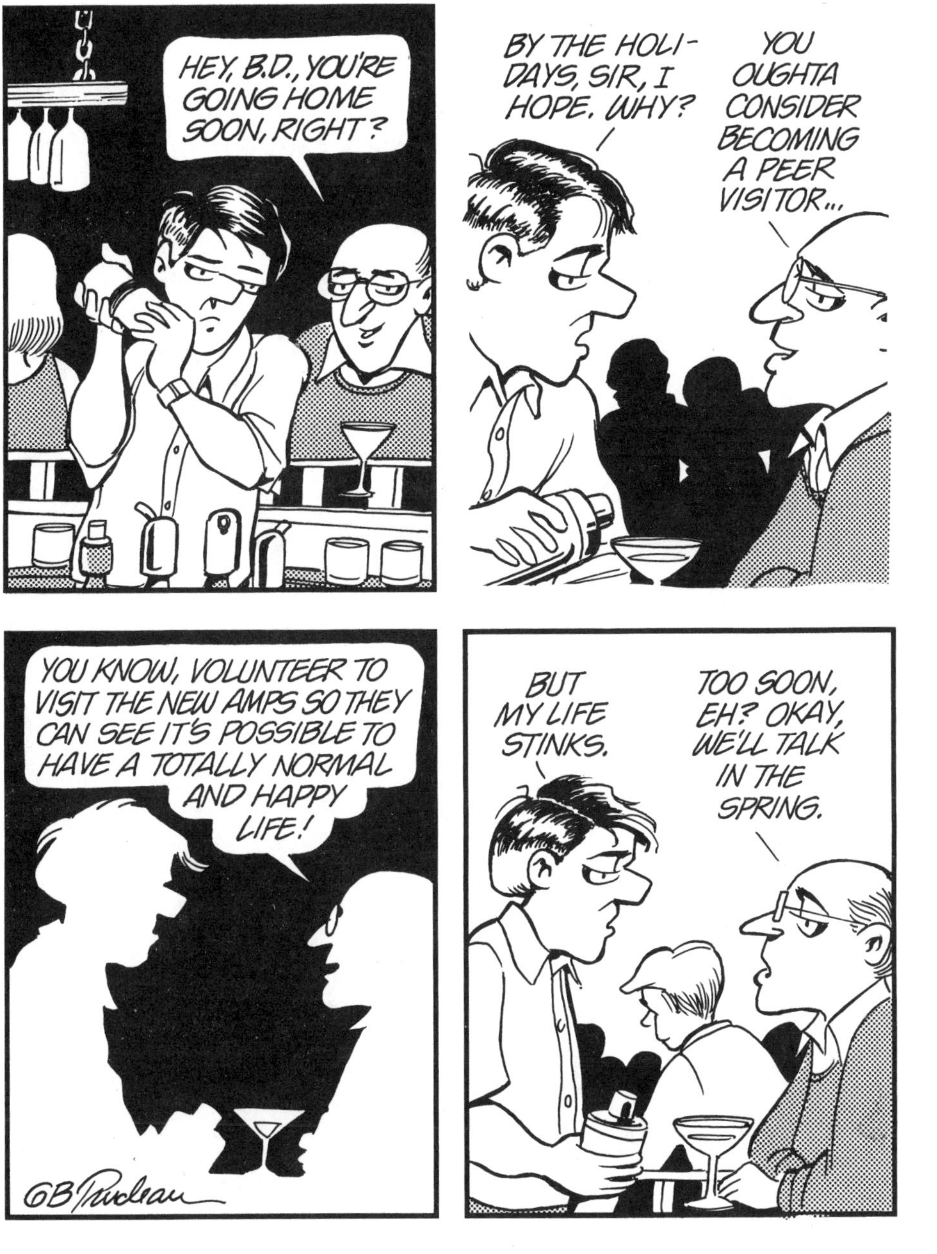
HEY, B.D., YOU'RE GOING HOME SOON, RIGHT?
BY THE HOLI-DAYS, SIR, I HOPE. WHY?
YOU OUGHTA CONSIDER BECOMING A PEER VISITOR...
YOU KNOW, VOLUNTEER TO VISIT THE NEW AMPS SO THEY CAN SEE IT'S POSSIBLE TO HAVE A TOTALLY NORMAL AND HAPPY LIFE!
GB Trudeau
BUT MY LIFE STINKS.
TOO SOON, EH? OKAY, WE'LL TALK IN THE SPRING.

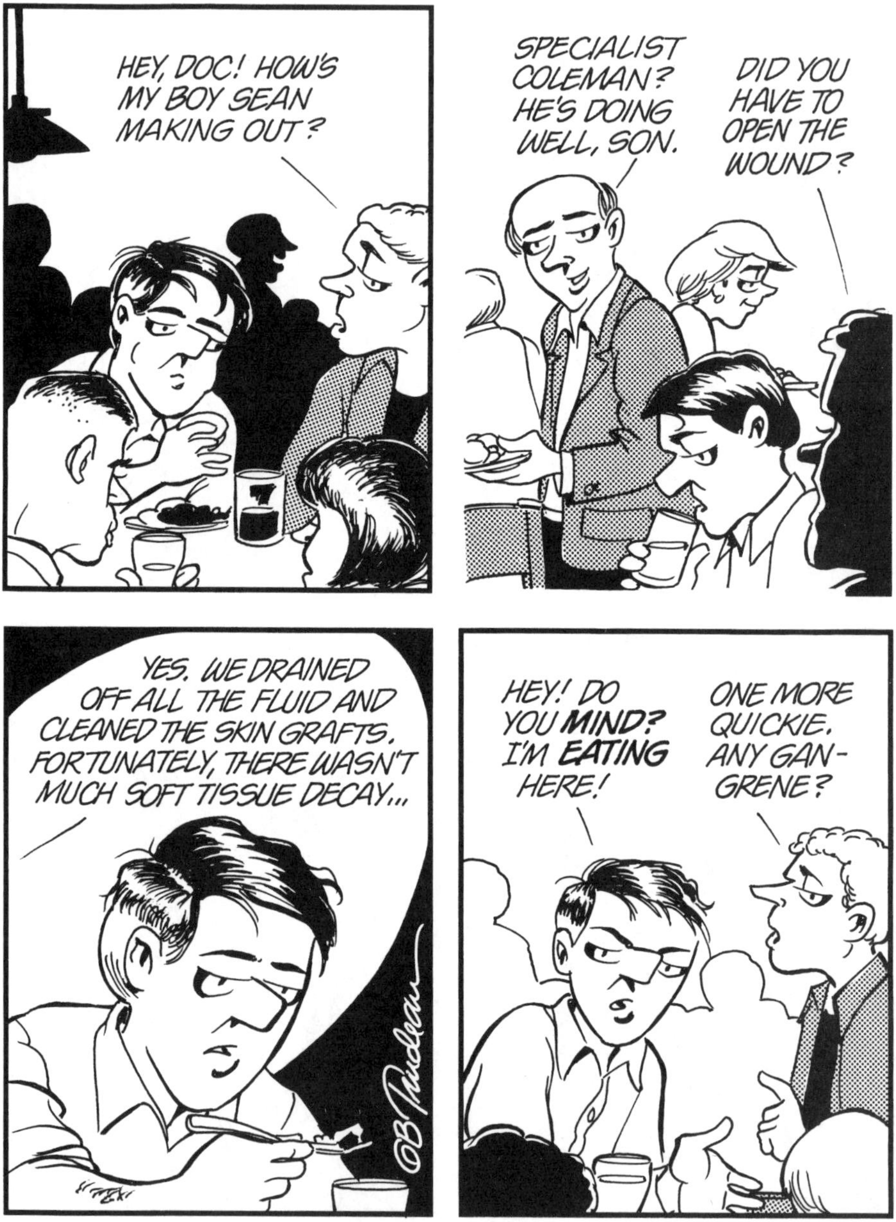
HEY, DOC! HOW'S MY BOY SEAN MAKING OUT?
SPECIALIST COLEMAN? HE'S DOING WELL, SON.
DID YOU HAVE TO OPEN THE WOUND?
YES. WE DRAINED OFF ALL THE FLUID AND CLEANED THE SKIN GRAFTS. FORTUNATELY, THERE WASN'T MUCH SOFT TISSUE DECAY...
©B Trudeau
HEY! DO YOU **MIND?** I'M **EATING** HERE!
ONE MORE QUICKIE. ANY GAN-GRENE?

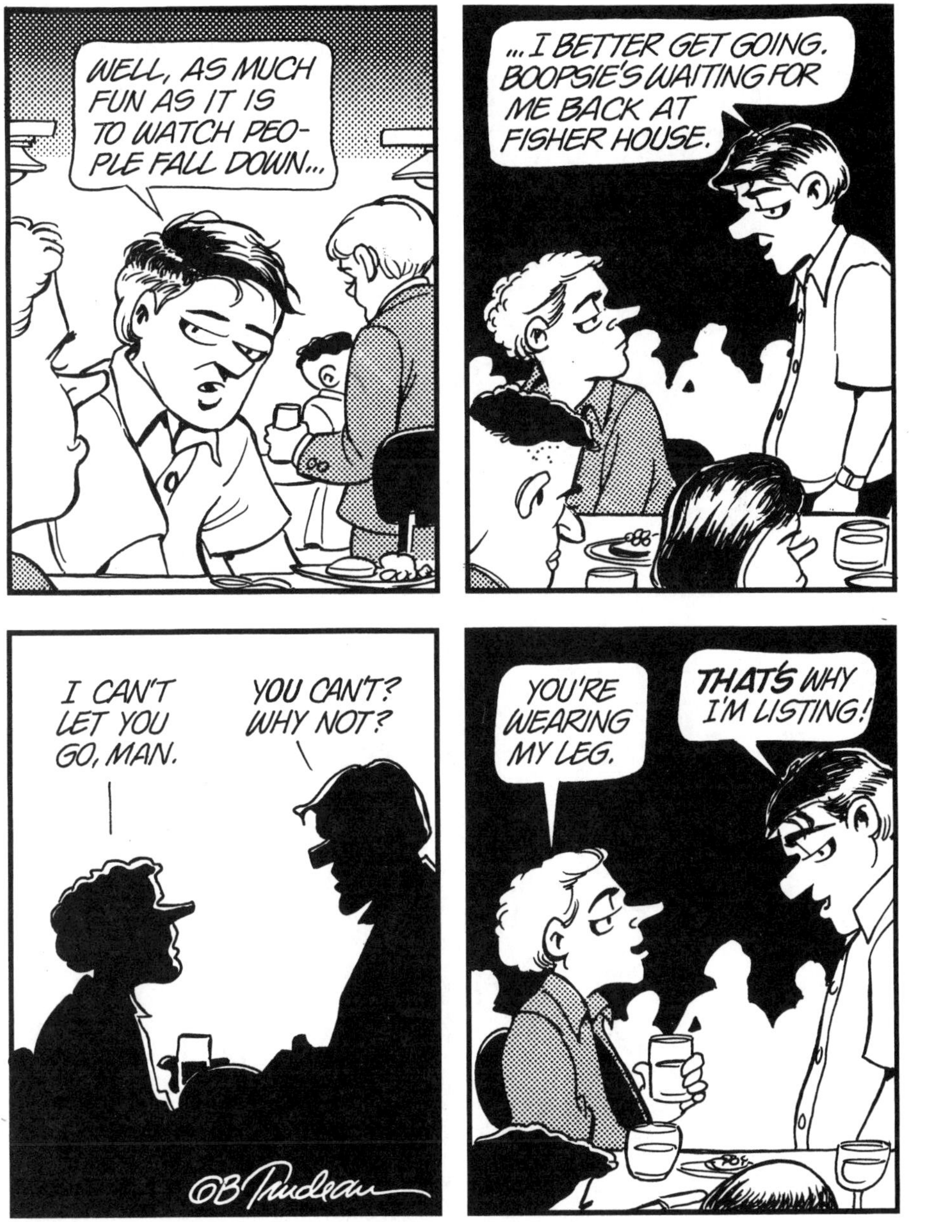
WELL, AS MUCH FUN AS IT IS TO WATCH PEOPLE FALL DOWN...
...I BETTER GET GOING. BOOPSIE'S WAITING FOR ME BACK AT FISHER HOUSE.
I CAN'T LET YOU GO, MAN.
YOU CAN'T? WHY NOT?
©B Trudeau
YOU'RE WEARING MY LEG.
THAT'S WHY I'M LISTING!

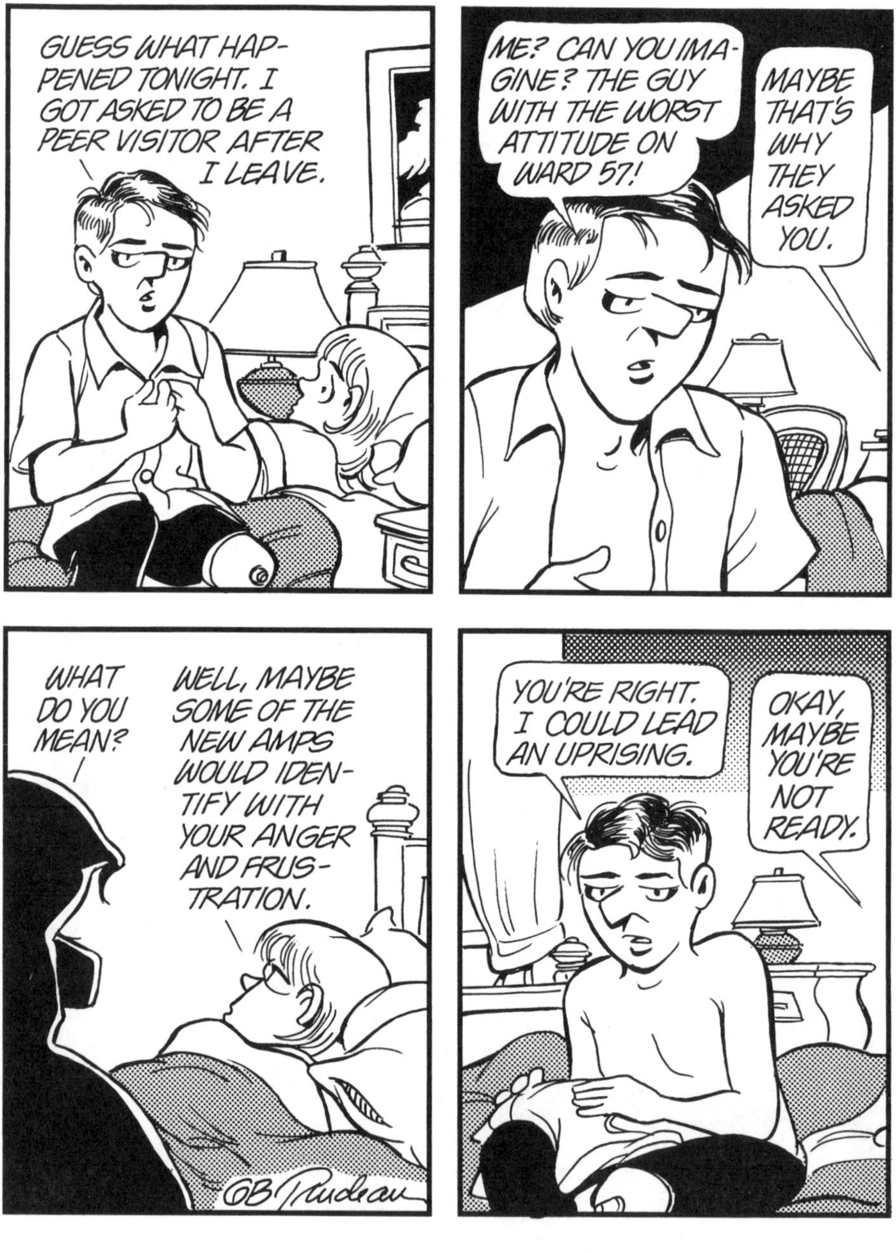
GUESS WHAT HAP-PENED TONIGHT. I GOT ASKED TO BE A PEER VISITOR AFTER I LEAVE.
ME? CAN YOU IMA-GINE? THE GUY WITH THE WORST ATTITUDE ON WARD 57!
MAYBE THAT'S WHY THEY ASKED YOU.
WHAT DO YOU MEAN?
WELL, MAYBE SOME OF THE NEW AMPS WOULD IDEN-TIFY WITH YOUR ANGER AND FRUS-TRATION.
GB Trudeau
YOU'RE RIGHT. I COULD LEAD AN UPRISING.
OKAY, MAYBE YOU'RE NOT READY.

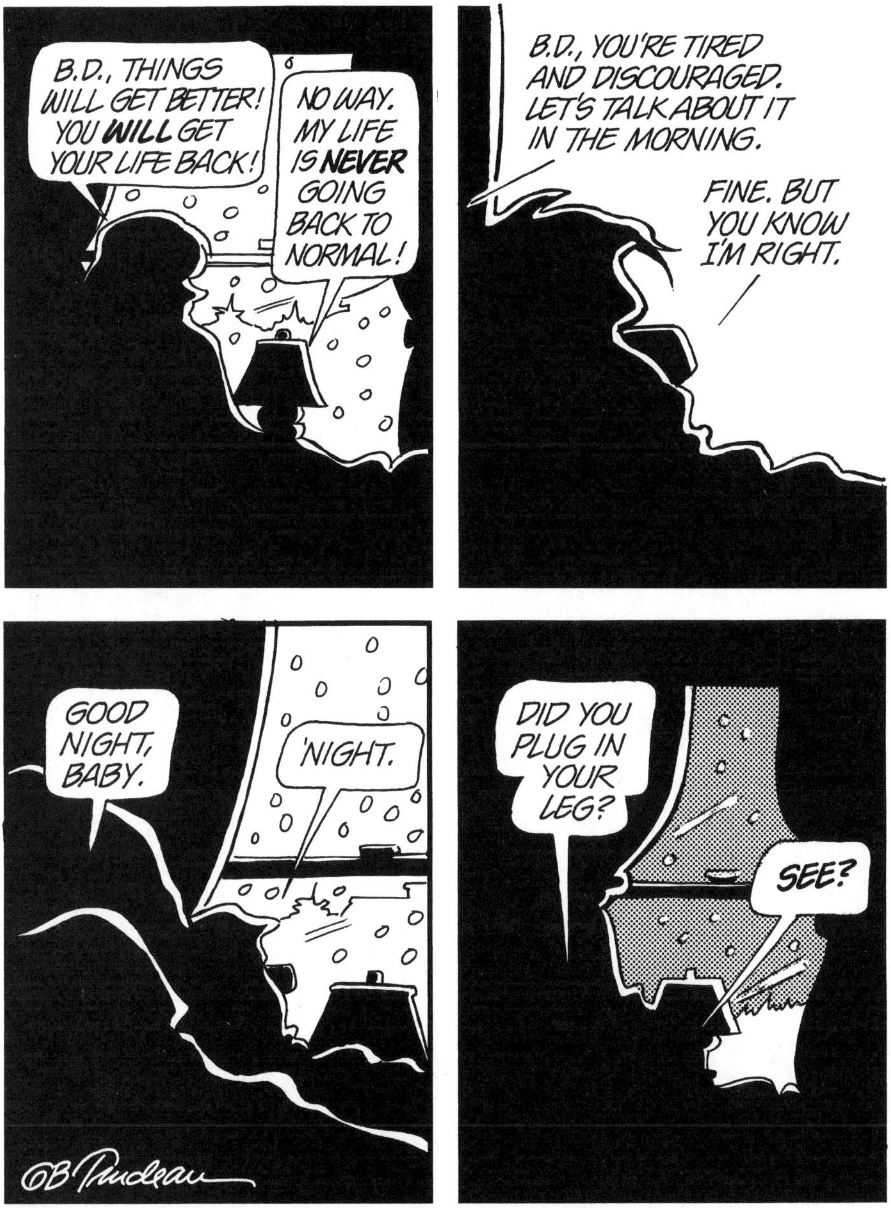
B.D., THINGS WILL GET BETTER! YOU WILL GET YOUR LIFE BACK!
NO WAY. MY LIFE IS NEVER GOING BACK TO NORMAL!
B.D., YOU'RE TIRED AND DISCOURAGED. LET'S TALK ABOUT IT IN THE MORNING.
FINE. BUT YOU KNOW I'M RIGHT.
GOOD NIGHT, BABY.
'NIGHT.
DID YOU PLUG IN YOUR LEG?
SEE?
©B Trudeau

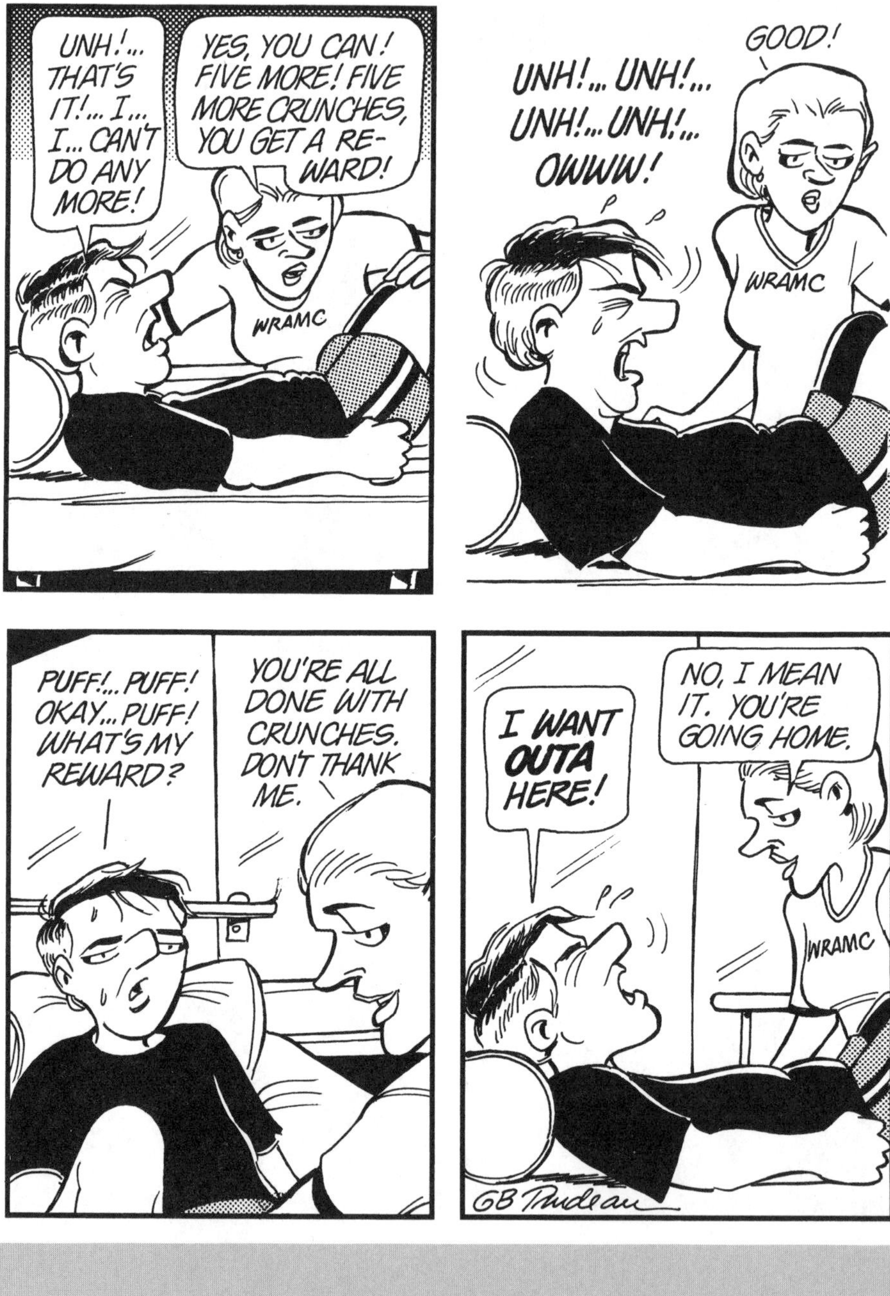
UNH!... THAT'S IT!... I... I... CAN'T DO ANY MORE!
YES, YOU CAN! FIVE MORE! FIVE MORE CRUNCHES, YOU GET A RE-WARD!
WRAMC
GOOD!
UNH!... UNH!... UNH!... UNH!... OWWW!
WRAMC
PUFF!... PUFF! OKAY... PUFF! WHAT'S MY REWARD?
YOU'RE ALL DONE WITH CRUNCHES. DON'T THANK ME.
I WANT OUTA HERE!
NO, I MEAN IT. YOU'RE GOING HOME.
WRAMC
GB Trudeau

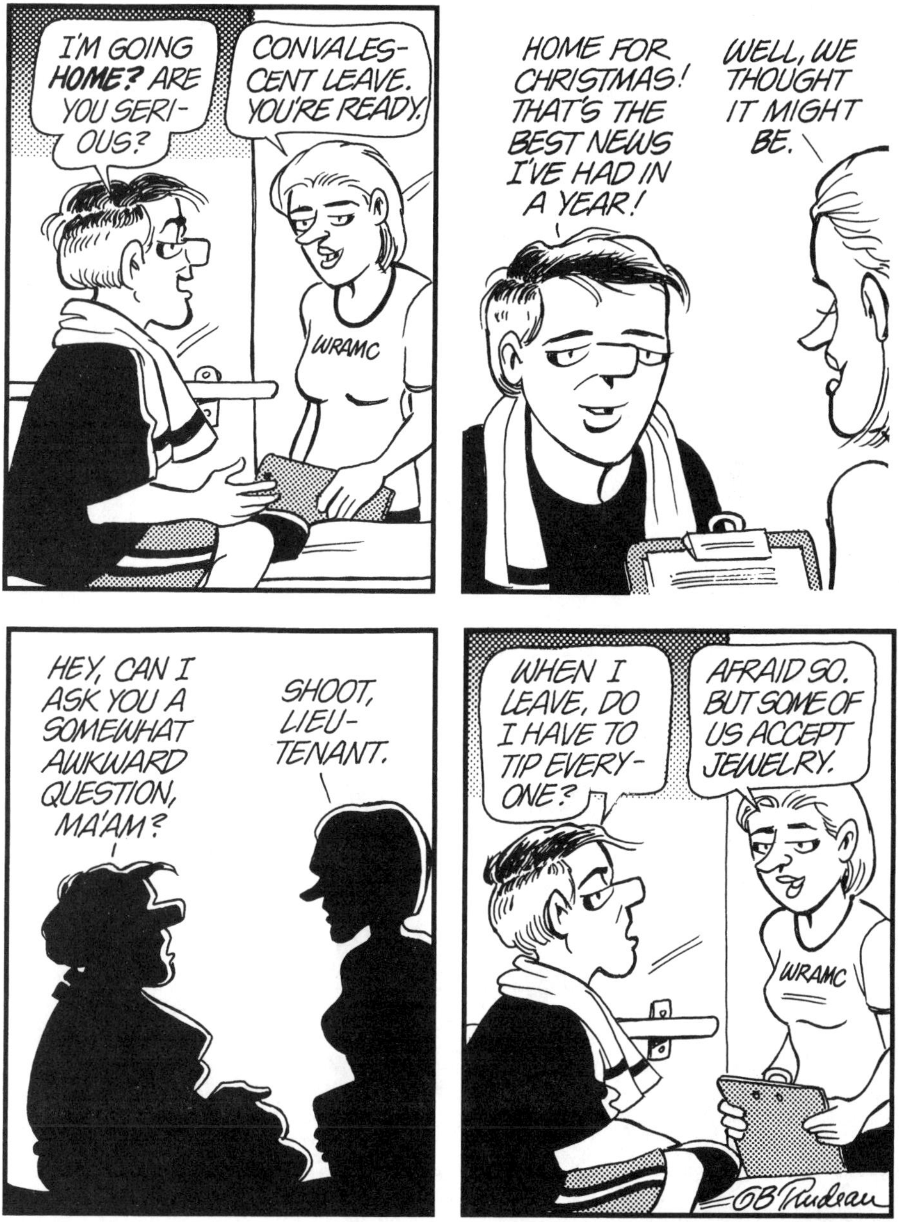
I'M GOING HOME? ARE YOU SERI-OUS?
CONVALES-CENT LEAVE. YOU'RE READY.
WRAMC
HOME FOR CHRISTMAS! THAT'S THE BEST NEWS I'VE HAD IN A YEAR!
WELL, WE THOUGHT IT MIGHT BE.
HEY, CAN I ASK YOU A SOMEWHAT AWKWARD QUESTION, MA'AM?
SHOOT, LIEU-TENANT.
WHEN I LEAVE, DO I HAVE TO TIP EVERY-ONE?
AFRAID SO. BUT SOME OF US ACCEPT JEWELRY.
WRAMC
GB Trudeau

YOU'RE COMING HOME? FOR REAL?
SAM! ZONK! HE'S COMING HOME!
©GB Trudeau
NOW THAT'S TIMING!
YOU'RE POSITIVE IT WON'T COLLAPSE?

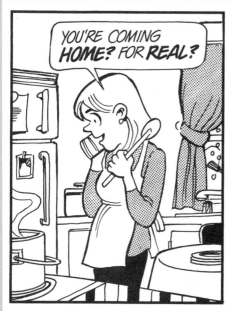

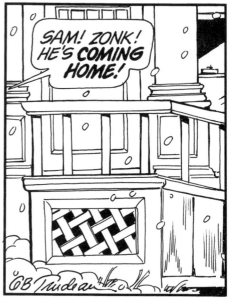

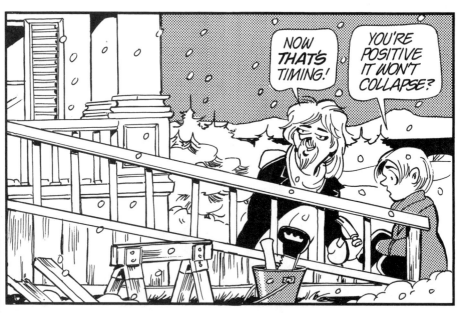

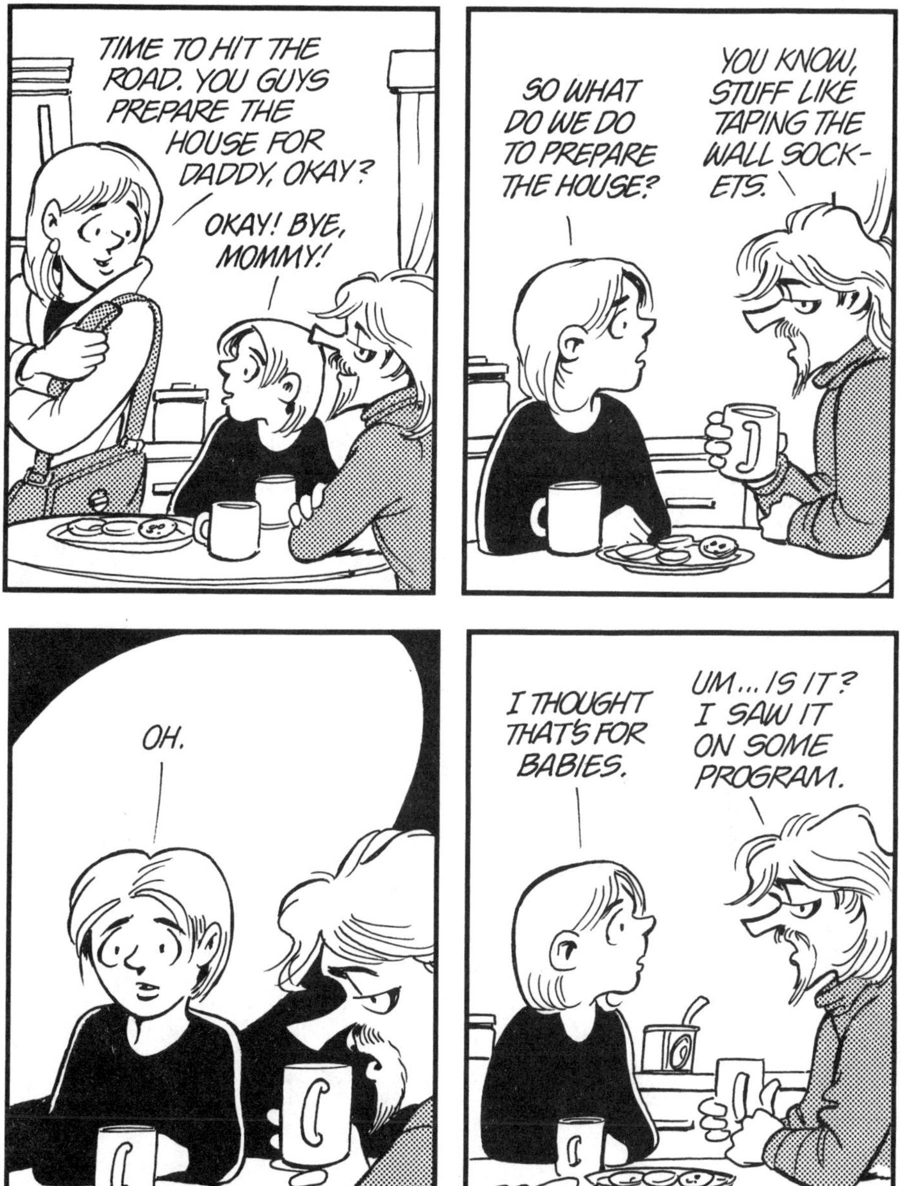
TIME TO HIT THE ROAD. YOU GUYS PREPARE THE HOUSE FOR DADDY, OKAY?
OKAY! BYE, MOMMY!
SO WHAT DO WE DO TO PREPARE THE HOUSE?
YOU KNOW, STUFF LIKE TAPING THE WALL SOCK-ETS.
OH.
I THOUGHT THAT'S FOR BABIES.
UM... IS IT? I SAW IT ON SOME PROGRAM.

MAYBE WHAT MOMMY MEANT BY PREPARING THE HOUSE FOR DADDY...
...WAS REARRANGING THE FURNITURE AND STUFF TO MAKE IT EASIER FOR A DISABLED PERSON.
OF COURSE!
FOR INSTANCE, THE STAIRS WILL BE A PROBLEM. SO WE MOVE THE BED DOWNSTAIRS! AND IF WE PULL THE FRIDGE NEXT TO IT, HE'LL HAVE ACCESS TO BEER!
LET'S DO IT!
OR IS THAT CODDLING HIM? CRAWLING UP STAIRS BUILDS ARM STRENGTH.
GB Trudeau

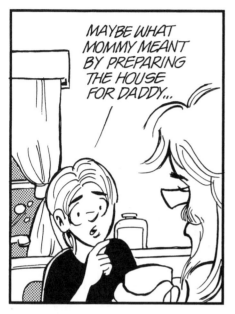

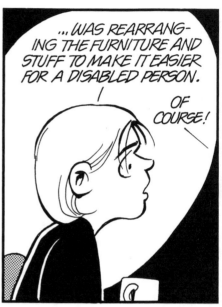

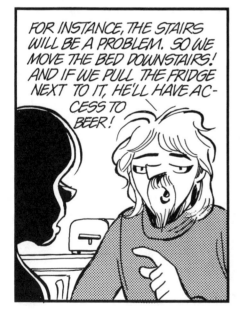

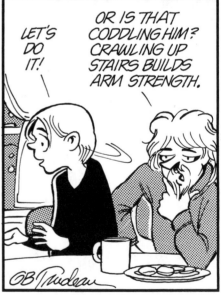

OKAY, I'VE WORKED IT OUT. WE HAVE TO MAKE THE HOUSE MORE FRIENDLY TO A DISABLED PERSON, RIGHT?

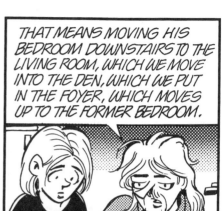

THAT MEANS MOVING HIS BEDROOM DOWNSTAIRS TO THE LIVING ROOM, WHICH WE MOVE INTO THE DEN, WHICH WE PUT IN THE FOYER, WHICH MOVES UP TO THE FORMER BEDROOM.

THE FOYER'S WHERE HIS BEDROOM IS NOW?

RIGHT!

GB Trudeau

WE HAVE TO GO UPSTAIRS TO LEAVE THE HOUSE?

A PRETTY SMALL SACRIFICE NEXT TO YOUR DAD'S, KIDDO.

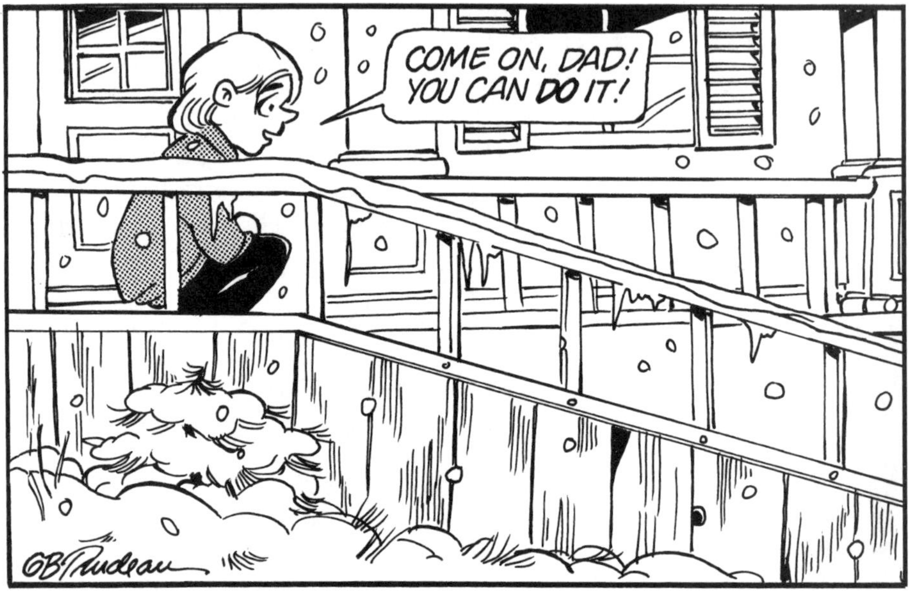
COME ON, DAD! YOU CAN DO IT!
GB Trudeau

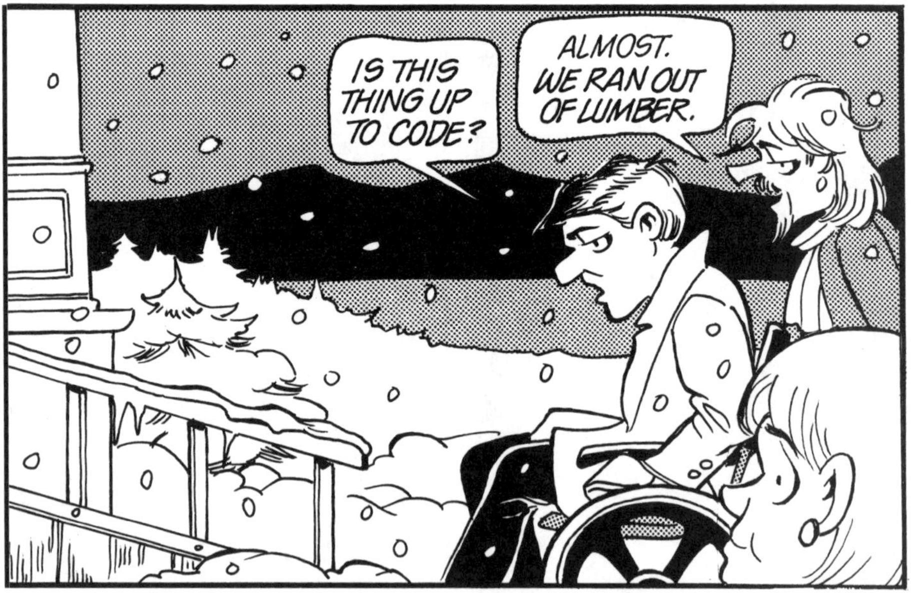
IS THIS THING UP TO CODE?
ALMOST. WE RAN OUT OF LUMBER.

WHOA... WHAT HAPPENED TO THE PLACE?
WE PREPPED IT FOR YOU!
TO MAKE THE HOUSE WAR-HERO-FRIENDLY, WE MOVED YOUR BED DOWN TO THE LIVING ROOM...
...RIGHT BESIDE THE TV AND ONLY STEPS FROM THE KITCHEN! WHAT DO YOU THINK?
THE BEDSIDE KEG IS A NICE TOUCH.
NO, IT'S NOT.
SURE IT IS!

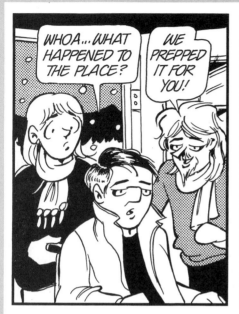

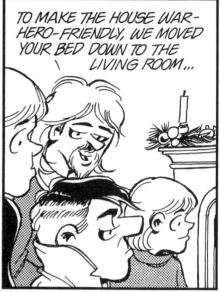

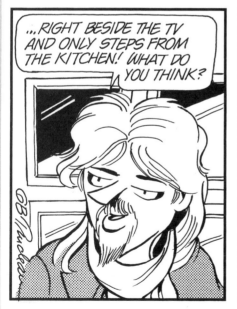

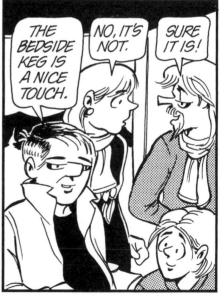

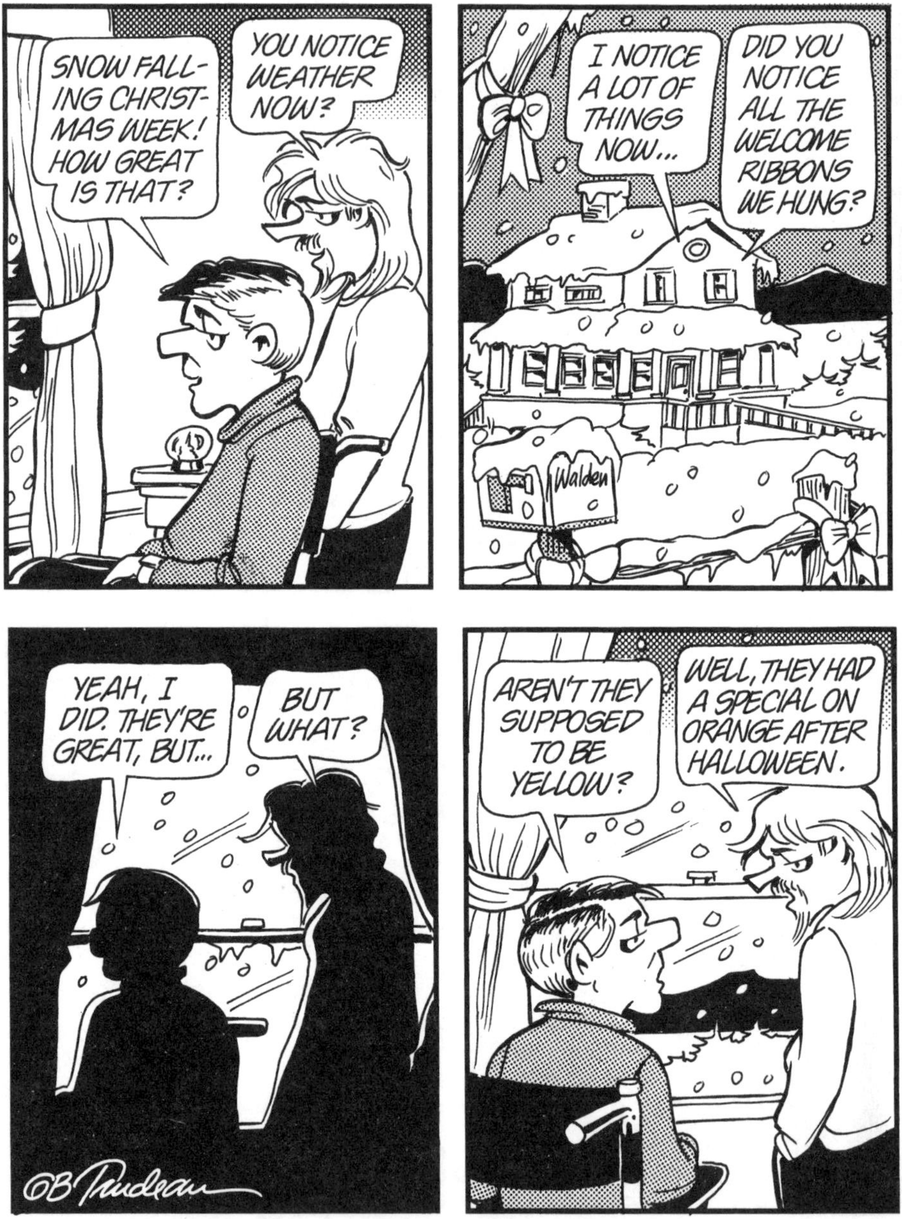
SNOW FALLING CHRISTMAS WEEK! HOW GREAT IS THAT?
YOU NOTICE WEATHER NOW?
I NOTICE A LOT OF THINGS NOW...
DID YOU NOTICE ALL THE WELCOME RIBBONS WE HUNG?
Walden
YEAH, I DID. THEY'RE GREAT, BUT...
BUT WHAT?
©B Trudeau
AREN'T THEY SUPPOSED TO BE YELLOW?
WELL, THEY HAD A SPECIAL ON ORANGE AFTER HALLOWEEN.

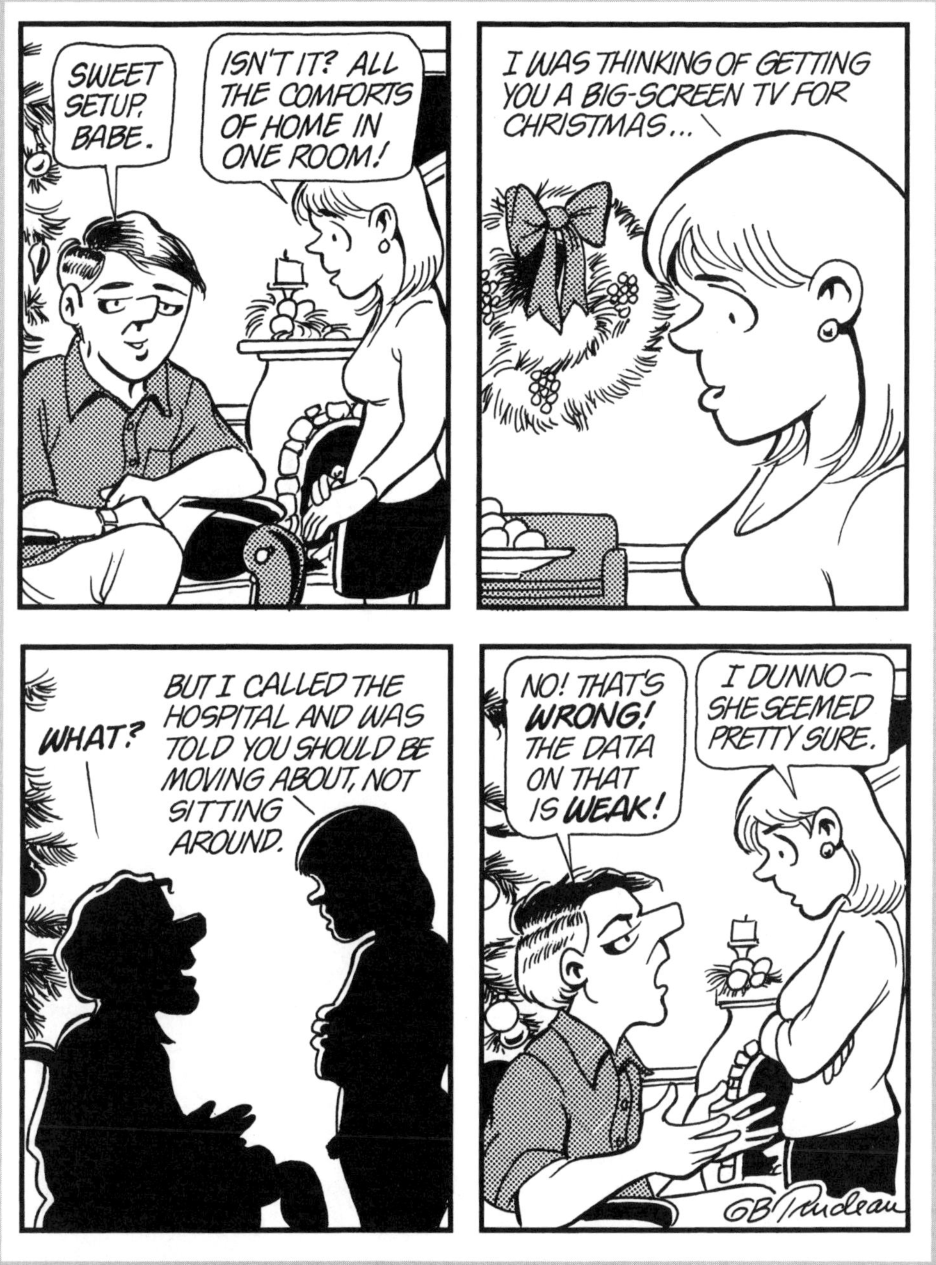
SWEET SETUP, BABE.
ISN'T IT? ALL THE COMFORTS OF HOME IN ONE ROOM!
I WAS THINKING OF GETTING YOU A BIG-SCREEN TV FOR CHRISTMAS...
WHAT?
BUT I CALLED THE HOSPITAL AND WAS TOLD YOU SHOULD BE MOVING ABOUT, NOT SITTING AROUND.
NO! THAT'S **WRONG!** THE DATA ON THAT IS **WEAK!**
I DUNNO—SHE SEEMED PRETTY SURE.
GB Trudeau

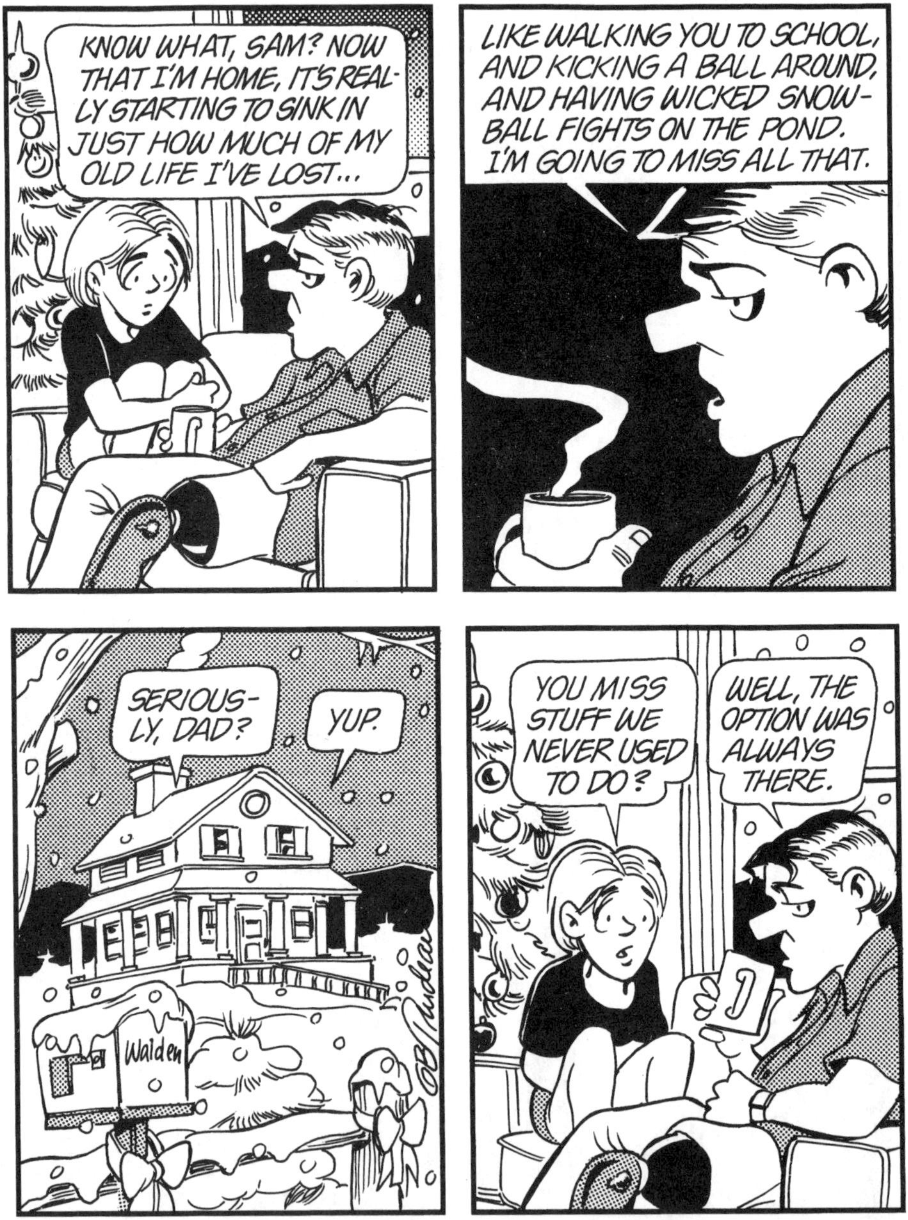
KNOW WHAT, SAM? NOW THAT I'M HOME, IT'S REALLY STARTING TO SINK IN JUST HOW MUCH OF MY OLD LIFE I'VE LOST...
LIKE WALKING YOU TO SCHOOL, AND KICKING A BALL AROUND, AND HAVING WICKED SNOWBALL FIGHTS ON THE POND. I'M GOING TO MISS ALL THAT.
SERIOUSLY, DAD?
YUP.
Walden
YOU MISS STUFF WE NEVER USED TO DO?
WELL, THE OPTION WAS ALWAYS THERE.

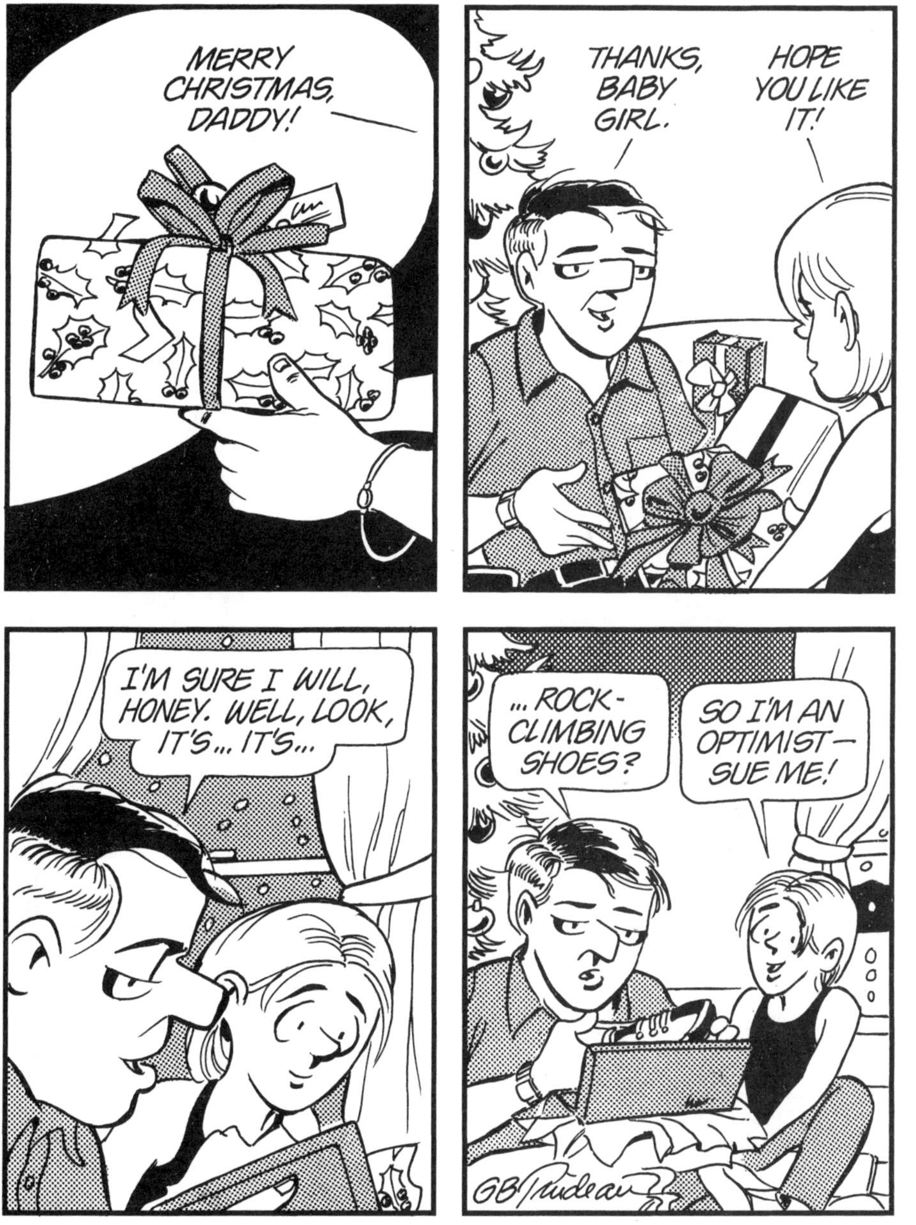
MERRY CHRISTMAS, DADDY!
THANKS, BABY GIRL.
HOPE YOU LIKE IT!
I'M SURE I WILL, HONEY. WELL, LOOK, IT'S... IT'S...
...ROCK-CLIMBING SHOES?
SO I'M AN OPTIMIST— SUE ME!
GB Trudeau

FISHER HOUSE
because A Family's Love
is Good Medicine

www.fisherhouse.org

A Fisher House is a "home away from home" for families of patients receiving medical care at major military and VA medical centers. As of this printing, there are thirty-three Fisher Houses located on seventeen military installations and seven VA medical centers, with another five houses in design. The program began in 1990 and has offered more than two million days of lodging to more than 70,000 families.

The Fisher House Foundation donates Fisher Houses to the U.S. Government. They have full-time salaried managers but depend on volunteers and voluntary support to enhance daily operations and program expansion.

Through the generosity of the American public, the foundation has expanded its programs to meet the needs of our service men and women who have been wounded. The foundation uses donated frequent-flier miles to provide airline travel to reunite families of the wounded and to enable our wounded heroes to go home to convalesce. They also help cover the cost of alternative lodging when the Fisher Houses are full.

For further information about these programs, to find out about volunteering, or to make a tax-deductible gift, go to their Web site at:

www.fisherhouse.org

You can also obtain information by writing them at:

Executive Director
Fisher House Foundation, Inc.
1401 Rockville Pike, Suite 600
Rockville, MD 20852

Phone: (888) 294-8560
E-mail: info@fisherhouse.org